Legal Practice Course Stage I Revision Guide

Written only by authors that were awarded distinctions on the LPC before embarking on training contracts with top City firms, the LPC Handbook is a Legal Practice Course revision guide that covers the following core modules:

- **Business Law, Business Accounts & Business Taxation**
- **Property Law**
- **Civil Litigation**
- **Criminal Litigation**
- **Professional Conduct & Regulation**
- **Wills & Administration of Estates**
- **Solicitors' Accounts**
- **Drafting & Skills**

What makes this revision guide unique?

Detail and coverage

This is the most detailed LPC revision guide available. It includes: a multitude of defined terms; comprehensive, yet easily digestible explanations of key concepts; a variety of procedure plans and flowcharts; and full statutory references throughout.

Presentation and format

This is the only full colour LPC revision guide on the market, which ensures that concepts can be introduced and explained as clearly and concisely as possible. The format has been developed over a number of years to facilitate readers' understanding and retention of information.

Illustrative examples

There are many practical, illustrative examples of exam questions and suggested answers throughout this guide, helping to clarify and contextualise the information contained in each topic.

is guide should be used in conjunction with your course notes, lectures and seminars. Use it to help clarify concepts and consolidate your understanding of topics when preparing r seminars and revising for exams. Take particular care to recognise elements of modules that you are expected to know for your course but are missing from this guide, and ncepts included that you are not expected to know. In addition, remember that the law is constantly developing. Significant changes may occur part way through your course and ese changes may or may not form part of the content which you are expected to know and apply in your exams. Always check whether the law has evolved since this guide was blished and know which version of the law your module leaders wish you to focus on. We do however print our guides on multiple occasions throughout the year so as to ensure ey remain as up-to-date as possible.

CityCareerSeries.com/Store amazon.co.uk **LPCHandbook.com**

CityCareerSeries.com

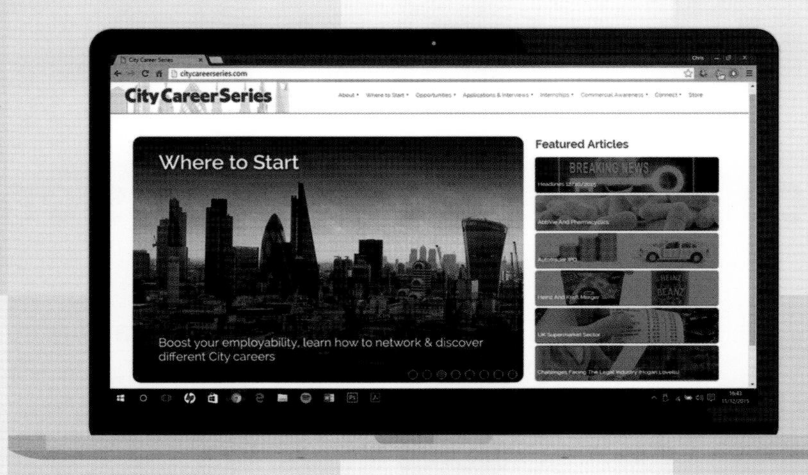

CityCareerSeries.com offers a multitude of high quality, concise and easy-to-understand tips, articles, videos and blogs:

- You will find information on boosting your employability, networking and the different types of firms and opportunities that you can apply for.
- The interactive (and syncable) calendar provides easy access to firm deadlines and links to application portals, whilst the firm profiles give you an insight into the range of City firms looking to hire graduates.
- You will find examples of application and interview questions that are typically encountered, complete with detailed suggestions of how to tackle them.
- Psychometric, situational judgement and e-tray tests are explained and techniques to help you approach them are suggested.
- Appropriate behaviour during internships is considered and hundreds of previous interns have offered an insight into their experiences whilst undertaking a variety of internships and placements at different City firms.
- Topical news stories are presented weekly, complete with explanations of why the stories may affect firms and their clients.
- Different industries have been analysed and the frameworks that can help you to conduct your own analysis of industries have been explained.
- An overview of the sources you should read to keep abreast of developments relevant to City firms and their clients has also been provided.

Social Media

 www.facebook.com/citycareerseries

 www.linkedin.com/company/city-career-series

 www.twitter.com/Career_Series

 City Career Series

Online Communities

Want to share tips and network with people at the same stage as you in the recruitment process?
Join one of our online communities!

- **Commercial Law Applicants**
  www.facebook.com/groups/commerciallawapplicants
- **Commercial Law Interns**
  www.facebook.com/groups/commerciallawinterns
- **Investment Banking & Finance Applicants**
  www.facebook.com/groups/investmentbankingandfinanceapplicants
- **Investment Banking & Finance Spring Interns**
  www.facebook.com/groups/investmentbankingandfinancespringinterns
- **Investment Banking & Finance Summer Interns**
  www.facebook.com/groups/investmentbankingandfinancesummerinterns
- **Operations, Risk & Compliance Applicants**
  www.facebook.com/groups/operationsriskandcomplianceapplicants
- **Technology Applicants**
  www.facebook.com/groups/technologyapplicants
- **Consultancy Applicants**
  www.facebook.com/groups/consultancyapplicants

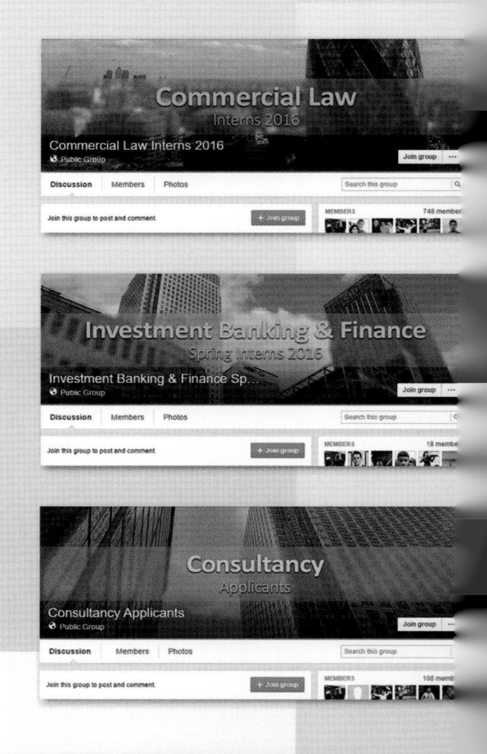

Contents

Introduction

This handbook offers a solid grounding in the general knowledge required for commercial law interviews and internships. It includes: a description of the role of commercial lawyers and different practice areas; consideration of key business, finance and economics concepts; an overview of key commercial law principles, documents and definitions; general interview advice relating to competency, commercial awareness and case study interviews; and much more.

This handbook is aimed primarily at students preparing for interviews and internships. For candidates who have not yet reached these stages, the Application, Interview & Internship Handbook provides guidance relating to boosting your employability, researching firms and careers, networking, structuring CVs and cover letters, answering application and interview questions, approaching psychometric tests, conducting yourself during internships and enhancing your commercial awareness.

How Should The Information In This Handbook Be Applied?

Many interviews involve firms providing candidates with case studies, business scenarios or articles. As part of the assessment, you may have to give a short presentation (these typically focus on business issues and/or how the firm can assist its clients), before then being questioned at length on various issues/discussion points. You may be questioned on topics such as: business performance, financing deals, mergers & acquisitions, investment options and the role of the firm/different departments. You may be provided with information on the background of a business; business accounts from recent years; press clippings about a business; information about a business' internal operations; and information on external developments relating to the industry in which the business operates.

Develop your business, finance and legal knowledge (elements of commercial awareness) so that you can demonstrate and apply strong commercial logic during case studies and commercial awareness interviews. If a client is considering purchasing another company, what are the different financing options and the corresponding advantages and disadvantages of each (see the *Financing A Deal* section)? How can such a transaction be structured (see the *How To Purchase A Business* section)? What are the primary risks and how they can be mitigated (see the *Buyer Protection* section)? How can the firm help (see the *Practice Areas* section)?

Demonstrate an ability to flexibly apply the concepts to the facts of the case study provided and assess in that particular case study which concepts are likely to be the most relevant and effective.

How Should You Use This Handbook To Prepare?

Please take this as only a basic guide. We encourage you to research into all the terms and concepts contained within in greater depth, as they are by no means definitive or guaranteed to be wholly or objectively accurate. Terms have been defined throughout, but many of these definitions are subjective and no consensus exists as to their precise definition. I have included information which I personally found to be useful in my interviews and internships, but I researched into the terms and concepts included in greater depth and read around the subjects to ensure my understanding was sufficient to intelligently discuss the concepts with interviewers and supervisors.

I recommend that you use this handbook as a framework around which interview preparation can be structured. If you decide to discuss the concepts contained within this handbook, you are likely to be tested on your application of them, both in fictitious case studies and in the context of real work, clients and industries. Rather than merely memorising/regurgitating the definitions and concepts contained within this handbook, ensure your understanding is strong. I was tested on many of the concepts after bringing them up in a variety of interviews and could not have succeeded had I not truly understood them.

Please do not be overwhelmed by the sheer volume of potentially brand new content contained in this handbook. I was not expected to know all of this information in any one interview; the concepts contained within were merely of use at some point throughout the 15+ interviews that I personally attended. In addition, I studied Law & Business at the University of Warwick, so firms may well have expected a slightly greater level of legal and business understanding from me than they would from candidates with no grounding in either discipline.

However, understanding the concepts contained within this handbook could give you an essential edge and is more important and valuable than simply recalling technical terms. Discussing them in the context of interview case studies, or with supervisors when they set you related work during internships, can lead to positive feedback in relation to your commercial awareness/interest. It is worthy to note that if you understand certain concepts but cannot remember the technical terms, this will not necessarily be a problem.

Opportunities In The Legal Profession

Training at a large, international commercial law firm is the best way to start your career if you want to work in the City and have an aspiration to handle very high value commercial transactions. In addition, you will be given fantastic opportunities to develop your soft skills and technical abilities (not to mention the boost it can provide to your CV). However, try not to lose sight of the fact that the legal profession offers a broad range of opportunities for employment.

If you went to a Russell Group university, you will have been exposed predominantly to large, international commercial law firms, as these are the firms that offer the greatest number of training opportunities (and can afford the fees charged by your universities to host large events!). Some top barristers' chambers may also promote themselves to students. This might have given you the impression that failing to secure a training contract or pupillage at a top-ranking firm means that your legal career is over before it has even started, or that your only option will be to train at a firm where the work is far less interesting, challenging and/or fulfilling. This is simply not the case. In fact, there are often benefits to training at smaller firms.

Regional firms, boutique firms and high street firms may not offer the same opportunities to work on transactions/disputes that are worth hundreds of millions (or billions) of pounds and span dozens of jurisdictions. However, smaller transactions/disputes may offer you the opportunity to get far more involved at a more junior stage. This is because there is less at stake financially, which typically means such deals are likely to involve fewer documents and parties (e.g. foreign legal counsel, external advisers etc.). If you're the kind of person that really gets a kick out of seeing a deal on the front page of The Financial Times, then perhaps smaller firms aren't for you. However, if having more control and (potentially) a greater overall impact on a deal gives you a greater sense of job satisfaction, then certainly consider all the options that are available. After all, you can experience plenty of academic challenge on matters that are not worth millions or billions.

If you are unsure of the type of law you want to practice, then look to train at a firm that has a wide range of practice areas; the more areas you try, the more likely it is that you will find the best fit for you. You might find that a firm that offers private client work as well as commercial work gives you the widest opportunity to explore different kinds of legal work and make an informed decision on your future. Sometimes people find when they start work that the practice area they always thought would be for them just doesn't suit and they end up (happily) doing something completely different.

Post-training, there are ample opportunities to work 'in-house'. This simply means working for a company rather than a law firm. For example, corporations (e.g. Apple), banks (e.g. J.P. Morgan) and private equity firms (e.g. Cinven) all have their own legal teams. These legal teams tend to carry out the company's day-to-day legal work, then bring in and co-ordinate/work alongside external legal advisers (e.g. Freshfields Bruckhaus Deringer) to help with larger transactions or disputes. Your work/life balance tends to be a little better working in-house, although the pay is typically lower (especially at a more junior level). In addition, you will only carry out your company's legal work, which may not appeal as much if you are the type of person that wants to work for dozens of different companies throughout the year (as would be the case at a large commercial law firm).

There are also a number of opportunities to work abroad. For instance, there are many firms based in tax-efficient jurisdictions (e.g. the Caymen Islands) that look to recruit English-qualified lawyers, although these firms usually require you to have accumulated a few years of post-qualification experience first. Some firms also offer opportunities to qualify into (or go on an extended secondment to) one of their international offices (and doing so doesn't always require you to take an additional legal qualification).

To summarise, keep an open mind, keep your eyes open, and try to use your research, internships and training contract to really think about which area of law suits you best and the type of firm at which you want to practice law in the long-term.

Which Undergraduate/Postgraduate Opportunities Are You Eligible To Apply For?

- Commercial law firms tend to offer insight days for 1st year students, although a select few offer 2 day or week-long experiences. Some firms also offer open days for students at any stage in their education (including graduates). These opportunities may include work-shadowing, group exercises and presentations from lawyers and graduate recruiters, but typically involve little or no responsibility.

- These opportunities may (depending on the firm) also lead to fast-track opportunities and at the very least, they provide evidence of your research and commitment to the career. This can therefore bolster your application for a full internship later on.

- Many firms then offer longer internships at Christmas, Easter and/or summer (timing can depend on whether you study Law and whether you are in your penultimate or final year of study). Candidates will usually sit in one or two departments during the internship and will have the opportunity to work with their supervisor and/or team on real work.

- If you receive a job offer, you will then have to complete the Legal Practice Course (LPC) followed by a period of "recognised professional training" (normally lasting for 2 years and referred to as a "training contract") before you become a qualified solicitor. Non-Law students will also have to complete the Graduate Diploma in Law (GDL) before embarking upon the LPC.

- Note that this may all change over the next few years however. The Solicitors Regulation Authority (SRA) is currently consulting stakeholders on the proposed introduction of a standardised "Solicitors Qualifying Examination" to replace the GDL and LPC.

We have produced a series of videos and articles that give you an insight into the recruitment process for commercial law firms and the range of opportunities that are available. These can be viewed at:

www.CityCareerSeries.com → Where To Start? → Introduction to Commercial Law

The interactive (and downloadable) calendar on our website provides easy access to a multitude of firm deadlines and links to application portals. This can be found at:

www.CityCareerSeries.com → City Firms & Deadlines → Calendar

We have put together a selection of firm profiles that give you an insight into the range of commercial law firms that offer insight experiences, internships and graduate roles. These can be found at:

www.CityCareerSeries.com → City Firms & Deadlines → Commercial Law

Acknowledgments

A special thank you to Sarah Cockburn, without whose continuous support and advice this handbook may never have materialised. A huge thanks to the City Career Series team (Carly Schogger, Nowtash Alsafar and Chris Phillips) for their incredible hard work, creativity and enthusiasm. A massive thank you to Claire Leslie (Warwick Law School Careers Consultant), Donna Schogger, Hugh Beale, Lauren Cooper, Frida Gundmark and Sean Markowicz for their extensive edits and invaluable suggestions. Thanks also to Christopher Stoakes for all his advice and support and for providing the inspiration for the City Career Series handbooks.

Thanks to all those that have supported me throughout this project, in particular Danny Schogger, Poppy, Tomisin Mosuro, Neel Sapat, Alice Toop, Kai Majerus and the lawyers that I met whilst interning for all their lectures, inspiration, proof reading, comments and suggestions. Thanks to Sean McCaffrey and Philip Dekker for helping me find my way into commercial law and to Jasmine Schembri for involving me in the university society that inspired this handbook. Thank you to Vinay Mistry (vinay@vinaymistry.com) for designing citycareerseries.com and Chris Phillips (www.cphillipsdesign.uk) - who deserves a second mention - for his endless patience and fantastic graphic design work. Thank you to all the members and the executive committee of Warwick Commercial Law Society for all the positive responses and useful feedback relating to earlier drafts of this handbook over the years.

Please note that the firms that have contributed to this handbook are only responsible for the information contained in their particular articles.

What Do Commercial Lawyers Do?

Commercial lawyers are expected to identify, anticipate and solve problems and disputes, mitigate risk and explain substantive, complex information to clients in a concise, easily digestible manner. On a day-to-day basis, this may involve providing legal or commercial advice, contributing to meetings and conference calls, researching, drafting and proof-reading documents, negotiating with other parties, devising ways in which to mitigate risk, structuring deals, managing transactions and conducting due diligence.

Key Practice Areas

Candidates are usually required to know the key practice areas and the work that each practice area typically undertakes. The way in which firms organise and label their practice areas varies and some firms have practice areas that others do not. This is a basic guide to some of the primary functions of the most fundamental practice areas.

Corporate

- Corporate lawyers generally focus on deal execution for clients. Work handled includes share sales, mergers, acquisitions and joint ventures. Corporate lawyers typically liaise with and co-ordinate other internal departments (e.g. the Tax, Competition and Employment departments), sourcing specialist expertise and advice to facilitate transactions when the need arises.

- The Corporate department produces key documentation necessary to execute transactions; advises bidders and targets on public takeover offers; advises sellers and purchasers on private acquisitions and disposals; advises individuals on potential equity (share) purchases; and offers general corporate advice concerning, for instance, contractual rights and logistics.

Banking / Finance / Capital Markets

- Banking lawyers advise clients on finance-related matters, such as accessing the capital required to finance transactions. Work can include: acquisition financing (to help one company purchase another); general corporate lending (if a company requires capital); project financing (e.g. for building a wind farm); infrastructure financing (e.g. for building an airport or high speed rail network); asset financing (e.g. for building a large commercial property); restructuring and insolvency work (if a business encounters financial difficulties or is declared bankrupt); and deals relating to the capital markets (for instance bond issues).

- Finance lawyers produce the documentation required for a client to, for instance: issue debt (e.g. bonds) in the debt capital markets; list on a stock exchange; and secure large loans from a lender or syndicate (group) of lenders. Lawyers may also conduct due diligence to: determine whether a borrower is likely to default on a loan; ascertain whether security can be taken over an asset to support a loan; and ensure financial transactions comply with relevant regulations.

Insolvency: a company is 'insolvent' when it cannot pay its debts in time, or when the total of its liabilities exceeds its assets. If a company becomes insolvent, it must cease trading.

Liabilities: legal responsibility for a particular problem, or in finance terms, outstanding debt.

Security: taking security over a borrower's assets can increase a lender's chances of receiving back its money if the borrower defaults on the loan. There are many types of security, including mortgages, fixed and floating charges and guarantees. Some of these are considered in more detail later in this handbook.

Guarantee: involves a guarantor (e.g. a parent company) making a legal promise to a lender that they will fulfil any outstanding financial obligations covered under the guarantee if the borrower (e.g. a subsidiary of the parent company) defaults on a loan.

Subsidiaries: subsidiaries are companies that are owned/controlled (or partially owned/controlled) by another company (known as the 'parent' or 'holding' company).

Dispute Resolution / Litigation / Arbitration / Mediation

- Lawyers in the Dispute Resolution department engage in or challenge disputes for clients; pre-empt and attempt to prevent conflicts arising; develop contingency plans; and undertake due diligence to ascertain whether a potential acquisition target has any outstanding litigation that may result in liabilities transferring to the buyer. Disputes lawyers may work on cases involving regulatory compliance, product or personal liability, the media (defamation claims for instance), insurance or commercial fraud. Cases occasionally reach trial, which may involve taking witness statements, bundling, appealing, negotiating a settlement, and at times advocacy.

- However, litigation can be costly, time consuming, distracting and damaging for a company's reputation (if negative press attention is garnered). Accordingly, clients may prefer to pursue alternate dispute resolution (ADR) methods such as arbitration and mediation as these are private and can be more flexible, quicker and cheaper to pursue than litigation (which involves the courts).

📖 **Arbitration**: a process used by parties to settle disputes. An impartial arbitrator (or panel) is nominated who may, if the parties so choose, be an expert in the field and thus be better placed than a judge to make an informed decision.

📖 **Mediation:** a process conducted confidentially that involves parties in dispute nominating a neutral third party (a facilitator) to actively assist them in working towards a mutually beneficial arrangement (with a view to avoiding a trial). The parties are in ultimate control of the decision to settle and the terms of the resolution. The facilitator is not a decision-maker; he/she merely helps the parties examine the problems.

Tax

- Almost every transaction will have tax implications. Tax lawyers may help to determine the way in which transactions should be structured (for instance whether clients should pursue share or asset sales) and the methods of financing that should be used for a transaction (cash reserves, debt or equity). Tax lawyers also liaise with HM Revenue & Customs and advise on tax disputes and investigations. This may involve consideration of whether tax schemes are illegal or abusive through analysing the many different statutes, rules and regulations that apply to tax, for instance the General Anti-Abuse Rule.

- Examples of ways in which firms can minimise their tax bill include: borrowing money from subsidiaries in more tax efficient jurisdictions and paying high interest rates in return; paying large franchise fees to franchisors based in more tax efficient jurisdictions; or paying inflated prices when acquiring goods from subsidiaries along the supply chain in more tax efficient jurisdictions.

- These strategies effectively enable companies to reallocate (or reroute) profits from subsidiaries (or other companies within the same group) in jurisdictions with high corporate tax rates to other subsidiaries (or companies within the same group) that exist (and thus pay tax) in jurisdictions offering more favourable tax rates. Consequently, there would be less profit available for taxation in jurisdictions with high tax rates.

📖 **Special Purpose Vehicle (SPV):** a legal entity (shell company) created to serve a particular function. Firms may include special purpose vehicles within their corporate structures to absorb financial risk or reduce tax liabilities, for instance through registering and operating them in tax havens such as the Cayman Islands or Luxembourg.

Commercial Property / Real Estate

- Real Estate/Commercial Property lawyers advise on the construction, acquisition, sale, transfer and financing of tangible assets such as buildings, land, other infrastructure, ships and planes. In addition to drawing up the relevant contracts, Real Estate lawyers may also work on: planning permission applications; large regeneration projects; leasing or licensing arrangements (usually of business premises); and property-related disputes. Real Estate lawyers often support the Corporate department on elements of deals that involve property.

- As part of the due diligence process, Real Estate lawyers may for instance have to ascertain: which assets are actually included in a deal; who owns the assets and whether the seller has the legal right to sell the assets; whether the assets are subject to a lease owned by a third party that will expire soon; whether the assets are subject to any undisclosed charges (for instance a mortgage) or interests (for instance a right of usage granted to a third party); whether the assets are in a satisfactory condition; and whether restrictions exist that, for instance, prohibit development upon any land involved.

Employment / Benefits / Pensions

- Advises on employment-related issues that arise in transactions such as mergers, takeovers, restructurings and insolvencies. In addition to drafting employment contracts, lawyers can advise on: remunerating or incentivising employees (for instance devising strategies relating to executive remuneration, such as offering shares to key employees); recruiting or retaining employees (for example, considering whether a key management team can leave if the company for which they work is acquired); disciplining or dismissing employees; sickness and maternity issues; and reorganisations. Employment lawyers may also engage in contentious employment-related disputes, concerning issues such as discrimination, unfair dismissal, or illegal soliciting of another company's employees. Pensions lawyers can facilitate the transfer of pension schemes, or conduct due diligence to ascertain whether the pension scheme of a proposed target is in too great a deficit.

Competition / Antitrust

- Competition lawyers advise clients on whether proposed transactions are likely to be classified as anti-competitive (for instance if they could create a monopoly). Work can involve analysis of allegedly anti-competitive agreements, mergers, state aid (where governments subsidise select companies) and cartels (an association of firms, manufacturers or suppliers engaged in a formal agreement to fix prices in particular territories and consequently restrict competition).
- The work involves much analysis of regulation in different jurisdictions and can require competition lawyers to sell to regulators why a proposed transaction will not result in a substantial lessening of competition (SLC). To do this, when analysing the companies and products involved competition lawyers must take into account many factors, including: the principle activities of companies involved; customer perceptions of the company (including its brand and marketing); the use or purpose of a product or service; the design or composition of a product; the ingredients or materials from which a product is derived; the price; whether the product is a substitute or complement; and the retail location of the product or service.

🕮 **Monopoly / Oligopoly:** where a firm (or a small group of firms in the case of an oligopoly) owns such a large share of its market that it has total (or substantial) control over trade within that market. A monopoly/oligopoly can arise where certain companies have a unique selling point that other companies struggle to compete against and/or entering the market involves significant costs/investment. The control afforded by a monopoly/oligopoly can therefore make it difficult for competitors to emerge. This can enable those with a monopoly (or those that are part of an oligopoly) to charge inflated prices, reduce the quality of their products (to cut costs) and/or refrain from innovating (improving the products), in the knowledge that consumers cannot purchase the same products from alternate suppliers. Monopolies/oligopolies may therefore be deemed anti-competitive and thus illegal, depending on the extent to which competition is reduced. This can be problematic if companies want to merge.

Intellectual Property (IP)

- Intellectual Property lawyers help clients to secure and protect IP rights such as copyright, patents and trademarks to prevent others profiting from their ideas, inventions and brands (or causing reputational damage). Exclusive rights over IP can afford clients a dominant market position and in the context of an acquisition, purchasers will typically want to ensure that the seller's IP rights are included in the sale. The seller could otherwise start up a similar business after the sale and compete with the purchaser.
- IP lawyers may advise on whether proposed actions could breach any existing IP rights. Work may include: applying for patents, initiating litigation against infringers of clients' IP rights, or helping to license IP rights to other parties in return for a royalty. The work involved at times requires a technical understanding of the product and consequently some IP lawyers come from Science or Maths backgrounds.

🕮 **Copyright (©):** protects original artistic, musical, literary and dramatic works that have been recorded in some form. Examples include recorded songs and the content of books. Also protects computer software.

🕮 **Patents**: protect inventions (including processes, devices and designs) that are novel and inventive, with an ascertainable use or application. Patents afford the holder exclusive rights over the patented subject matter. Patents for instance protect the technology used to create Dyson vacuum cleaners and Apple iPhones.

🕮 **Trademarks (™):** protect signs and symbols (such as logos and brands) capable of graphic representation that distinguish different goods. Examples include the Coca Cola logo, McDonalds golden arches and Nike tick. If a trademark has not been infringed, but the overall impression of a product indicates it is a copy of a competitor's product, this is known as 'passing off' and can still result in liability against the perpetrator.

🕮 **Geographical Indicators (GI):** names or signs that identify goods as originating in specific geographical locations, where a given quality, reputation, production method or other characteristic is attributable to that origin. For example, goods can only be labelled 'Darjeeling Tea' or 'Champagne' if produced in specific locations.

CLIFFORD CHANCE

Careers

WHERE BRIGHT MINDS MEET

COMMERCIAL LAW HANDBOOK

TOGETHER WE ARE CLIFFORD CHANCE

Choosing a career in Law brings with it a number of important decisions, and one of those is which Practice Area to qualify in to. Here a mixture of Trainees, Newly Qualified Associates, and Associates share their experiences of the various Practice Areas at Clifford Chance.

CAPITAL MARKETS

Leland Hui
(Trainee)

An average day in Capital Markets might involve drafting a range of different transaction documents; making submissions to the UK Listing Authority, handling due diligence; and/or communicating with lawyers in other jurisdictions. I would recommend Capital Markets to future trainees as the work is fast-paced with quick turnaround times, meaning that it is possible to see a number of transactions from start to finish during your time in the seat. This makes for a more 'complete feel'. There is also variation within the work and it is easy to get fully immersed in the transactions, even as a trainee.

TAX, PENSIONS AND EMPLOYMENT

Robert Sharpe
(Senior Associate)

The following makes the Tax practice a great place to work: the broad and varied range of work which we do, the collegiate atmosphere, and the fact that the work is interesting and intellectually stimulating. Tax issues have received a lot of press attention recently and I have been lucky enough to work on very high profile matters, including advising on the new Sugar Levy on the soft drinks industry. As well as providing tax advice on transactions, I am also part of the Tax Disputes team, which involves guiding clients through tax litigation and advising them on how to respond to tax investigations and audits, whether instigated by HMRC or foreign tax authorities across the world.

REAL ESTATE

Melissa Sykes
(Associate)

Real Estate gives trainees the opportunity to work on a variety of different transactions, both pure real estate and corporate. You also work closely with other specialist teams such as Environment & Planning and Construction which means that every matter involves a collaborative approach. A highlight includes running a procedure under the Rights of Light Act 1959, which involved corresponding with the Upper Tribunal (Lands Chamber) and the City of London Land Charges department as well as investigating title to land in North Wales in relation to an offshore wind farm. I also had the opportunity to get involved in marketing through the preparation of a Cross Border Commercial Real Estate Guide.

FINANCE

Lewis Cymbal
(Associate)

The work undertaken in Finance is incredibly diverse. Given the multi-jurisdictional elements of such transactions, interaction with foreign law, overseas offices & external counsel is frequent and often a daily occurrence. I chose to qualify into the Restructuring & Insolvency Finance department because no one day seems the same as the next! It is a very commercial area of law to be involved in which I enjoy, whilst also being very academic and intellectual. I have experienced a variety of work on transactions concerning the rescheduling and restructuring of debt, and generally advising companies and creditors on approaches to restructuring, including the refinancing of facilities and amendment of existing documentation, as well as the enforcement of security.

L&DR

Anna Peace
(Associate)

The best aspect of working in L&DR is representing a number of the most prestigious global brands and multinational corporations in major disputes. Notwithstanding the nexus with the English Courts, most of the matters are multi-jurisdictional. The skills gained are easily transferable to other areas of law. Moreover, the department allows to hone one's advisory, research, analytical, organisational, drafting and communication skills. The department also presents the opportunity to work on high profile and precedent-making cases.

CORPORATE

Elliot Hirst
(Associate)

If you want to know what it's like to be involved in the world's biggest transactions, working with experts in their fields and gaining a great commercial understanding of the market and what clients want, there's nowhere better. I chose to qualify in the Corporate (M&A) department because the work is extremely engaging and rewarding when a deal closes – especially if it's a well-publicised deal. I also enjoyed the sense that each day is different and you can come in and find out that something completely new and interesting has come up. The range of work you undertake includes drafting, liaising with clients and overseas counsel, organisational and management work on a transaction and the all-important completion aspects.

Key Commercial Law Principles

This section gives a very brief (and oversimplified!) overview of some of the key commercial law principles that can be relevant when working as a commercial lawyer. It is unlikely that you would be expected to understand any of these principles in great detail during interviews and internships. However, understanding the basic principles could help you to create a good impression with interviewers and with supervisors during internships.

Contracts

Contracts form a key part of the commercial world. Buyers and sellers bind themselves to transactions through Sale and Purchase Agreements (SPAs). Employees and employers set out their respective duties and responsibilities in employment contracts. Lenders and borrowers set out their rights and obligations in loan agreements. Arrangements discussed later in this handbook such as licensing, franchising and outsourcing are governed by contracts. Without contracts (and the law governing the enforcement of contracts), the commercial world would have to function solely on trust, which would likely discourage people from transacting with one another.

Sale And Purchase Agreement (SPA): a legal contract that describes the outcome of key commercial and pricing negotiations and when signed, obligates a buyer to buy and a seller to sell a product or service. Examples include agreements to buy products and agreements to buy companies.

Share Purchase Agreement: contractual agreement to buy shares in a company.

How Is A Contract Formed?

Contracts can be formed in a number of different ways. Contractual terms are typically set out in a document and signed by the relevant parties. However, contracts can also be created by any number of other means (e.g. through oral agreement and electronic communication) so long as the basic elements required to create a contract exist. The key elements are:

Offer → **Acceptance** → **Consideration** → **Intention**

1. **Offer**

   - One party must make a clear offer to the other party. The terms of the offer must be certain and the offer should indicate that the offeror (the person making the offer) is genuinely prepared to proceed with the transaction if their offer is accepted.
   - You probably make 'offers' on a daily basis, although you may not realise that this is what you have been doing. For instance, when you go into a shop and approach the cashier with a product that you wish to buy, this constitutes an 'offer' to buy that product (assuming that you do not try to negotiate the price).

2. **Acceptance**

   - The offer must be *unconditionally* accepted by the offeree (the party that received the offer) and acceptance must correspond completely with the terms of that offer. 'Acceptance' has not occurred for these purposes if the offeree specifies qualifications/conditions to their acceptance or introduces different terms (e.g. a different price, delivery date or quantity). Instead, this would likely constitute a 'counter-offer', which the law dictates will void the original offer.
   - Acceptance must be communicated (by words or conduct) and must take place before the offer in question is withdrawn by the offeror or lapses. An offer will lapse if (a) the offeror specifies a time limit during which acceptance must take place and this time limit expires; or (b) if no time limit is specified by the offeror, after a 'reasonable' period of time.
   - There are complex rules governing the precise time at which acceptance is deemed to have taken place (timing can depend on the method by which acceptance is communicated, for instance by post or fax), but further discussion of this is outside the scope of this handbook.

3. Consideration

- The 'consideration' requirement in this context means that something of value must flow from *each* party to the other. If I promise to give my laptop to a friend for free, that friend has not given any consideration for my promise. My friend therefore cannot sue me for breach of contract if I do not then give him/her the laptop. However, if I promise to give my laptop to a friend *in exchange* for that friend promising to (for instance) give me money, give me their car or paint my house, then this would satisfy the 'consideration' requirement. It does not matter if the goods/services to be exchanged are of different value.

4. Intention to create a legal relationship

- The parties to a contract must be shown to have had the requisite intention to be legally bound to perform their obligation(s) under the contract. In commercial agreements (e.g. agreements between two businesses or agreements between businesses and customers), the presumption is that where (a) an offer is made; (b) acceptance has occurred; and (c) consideration exists, the parties *intend* to be legally bound.

- In contrast, in social arrangements (e.g. where a husband promises to clean the kitchen in exchange for his wife doing the shopping), the presumption is that neither party intends to create a legally binding agreement and thus no intention to create legal relations exists.

To place this in context, let's use the example of buying a chocolate bar in a supermarket. There is no signed document setting out a contract, however a contract is formed once the purchase is complete.

1. **Offer:** a valid offer is made if you offer to buy a chocolate bar in a supermarket at the price advertised.
2. **Acceptance**: acceptance has occurred once the cashier scans the product and accepts your money.
3. **Consideration:** the 'consideration' requirement is satisfied as you are paying (or promising to pay) money, whilst the supermarket is promising to transfer the chocolate bar to you.
4. **Intention:** the presumption is that you and the supermarket intended to enter into a legally binding contract, as the transaction is taking place in a commercial context (although you may not be thinking this explicitly at the time!).

Contractual Terms

The terms of a contract can be used to protect the respective parties. The purchaser of a chocolate bar is entitled to assume that the chocolate inside the wrapper is edible, that the flavours advertised on the wrapper are reflected in the taste, that the chocolate bar is not stale etc. So how do contractual terms protect the parties?

Implied Terms

Even if these terms are not expressly set out in the contract (which may very well be the case if the contract is agreed orally), the law will 'imply' certain terms into the contract. 'Imply' for these purposes means that the contract 'is to be treated as including' certain terms (even if it does not expressly do so). Examples of such implied terms are set out below.

1. The product must conform with its description

- If the packaging describes a certain product, then there is an implied contractual term that the contents of the packaging will contain that product. If this is not the case (e.g. a bottle labelled 'shampoo' actually turns out to contain toothpaste) then the supplier has breached this 'implied' contractual term.

2. The product is of satisfactory quality

- The meaning of 'satisfactory' will depend, for instance, on the description applied to the product (e.g. 'luxury', 'basic', 'shatterproof') and the price paid for that product (you would generally expect more expensive products to be of a higher quality). The goods must essentially be free from defects and fit for the purpose for which products of that description are commonly supplied.

- For instance, there is an implied contractual term that a chocolate bar should be edible; a new computer should have a reasonable battery life, run at a reasonable speed and work with the internet; a table should not spontaneously collapse etc.

Express Terms

Parties can (and often do in more complex commercial transactions) negotiate more precise terms and expressly include these in the contract. Parties may specify particular payment methods, delivery dates or alterations to products (e.g. upgrading a computer hard drive or shortening the sleeves of a shirt) in the contract.

Parties may also specify a special purpose that the product must serve. For instance, if a party purchases a swimming pool primarily for the purpose of diving off of a 10 metre high diving board, that party can specify that the pool must be 5 metres deep or 'sufficiently deep to dive into head first off of a 10 metre diving board'. Such terms would not necessarily be *implied* by law, as the law will generally only imply that products are fit for the purposes for which they are commonly supplied (and swimming pools are *commonly* supplied for swimming, not diving into off of 10 metre high diving boards).

Allocation Of Risk

Parties may also agree to allocate risk in a certain way. For example, if a seller based in the United States is selling a classic car to a buyer based in China and plans to ship the car to that buyer, who loses out if the car falls off of the ship in the middle of the sea? The parties can agree (in contract) the point at which the *risk* passes from the seller to the buyer. For instance, risk could pass when the car is loaded onto the ship in the United States, when the ship docks in China, or when the car is actually *received* by the buyer. You would be surprised how many legal disputes have arisen in respect of the meaning of 'received' in such contexts (but this level of detail is outside the scope of this handbook).

Warranties (statements of existing fact), undertakings (promises to take certain action in the future) and indemnities (promises to reimburse the other party if certain costs arise) can also be included in the contract to allocate/mitigate risk. Breach of these can result in the party that committed the breach having to pay damages (compensation) to the other party. These clauses are explained in more detail in the 'Buyer Protection' section of this handbook.

There are other ways in which businesses can mitigate risk when contracting with one another. For instance, if a supplier provides products on credit (meaning that payment is not required until a future date), a 'retention of title' clause in the agreement to supply the products could enable that supplier to retrieve those products if the firm to which the goods were supplied goes bankrupt without paying. In addition, a 'force majeure' clause can protect the parties if something unexpected were to prevent either party from fulfilling their obligations under the contract.

📖 **Retention Of Title Clause:** in a contract for the sale of goods, a retention of title clause ensures that title to (ownership of) the goods remains vested in the seller until the buyer fulfils certain obligations (typically payment). If the buyer goes bankrupt before paying for the goods, the seller can subsequently retrieve back the goods from the liquidator, as the passing of ownership in the goods (from the seller to the buyer) is conditional on payment being made by the buyer.

📖 **Force Majeure Clause:** predetermines the allocation of risk and frees each party from liability if specified circumstances beyond the control of the parties arise that prevent either party from fulfilling their obligations. Examples of such circumstances include strikes, riots, wars, or acts of god (including hurricanes, floods or volcanic eruptions).

Breach Of Contract

Here is a simplified summary of the law relating to breach of contract: if Party A breaches a contract with Party B, Party A must typically pay sufficient damages (compensation) to Party B to place Party B in the position he/she would have been in had Party A not breached the contract. This will usually involve Party A giving Party B a refund (or a replacement product) plus additional compensation for any costs incurred by Party B in relation to the transaction (e.g. the cost of having the product delivered).

Commercial Considerations

It is worth remembering that the commercial world is not governed *solely* by contracts. There are other commercial factors that may influence how parties transact together or how a party chooses to act when another party breaches a contract. For instance, a manufacturer may provide a refund for a product that a retailer or consumer is unhappy with (even if that manufacturer has not breached any contractual terms) in order to maintain a good commercial relationship with that retailer/consumer and/or maintain a reputation for good customer service.

Security

What Is 'Security'?

Security is an essential form of protection for lenders. When giving a loan, a lender may take 'security' over a borrower's assets in order to increase its chances of receiving back its money in full if the borrower defaults on the loan (fails to repay the loan as agreed), thus making lenders feel more *secure*. A borrower will offer security to persuade a lender to lend, or to persuade a lender to charge lower interest rates on the loan (in recognition that there is a lower risk of that lender not receiving back the money lent in full). 'Security' in this context refers to a right given by a borrower to a lender. This right usually relates to some (or all) of the borrower's assets, and typically entitles the lender to sell enough of those assets to repay itself if the borrower fails to repay the loan as agreed.

- When the lender takes such action, this is known as the lender 'enforcing' its security, i.e. invoking the pre-agreed right to sell the asset(s) and retain some or all of the proceeds. There still exists a risk that an asset over which security is taken will decrease in value to the extent that the secured lender would not fully recoup the money it is owed if the borrower defaults and that asset is sold. Lenders may therefore take security over assets worth more than the loan.

- If a lender invokes its right to sell the relevant asset(s), it must however return any excess proceeds to the borrower once it has recouped the amount it is owed. Note that the lender can *only* invoke its right to sell the borrower's assets if pre-agreed circumstances arise, most notably if the borrower defaults on the terms of the loan (e.g. fails to make an interest payment to the lender on time).

Over Which Assets Can Security Be Taken?

Security can be taken over a variety of assets. A purchaser of a home gives a lender a mortgage (this is a type of security) over his or her house in exchange for a loan. In simple terms, if that purchaser fails to repay the lender as agreed, the mortgage (security) entitles the lender to sell the house and repay itself out of the sale proceeds. In larger commercial transactions, there may be multiple lenders that collectively provide a loan (a 'syndicated' loan), and the amounts lent may be in the hundreds of millions rather than the hundreds of thousands. However, the basic premise is the same.

> **Syndicated Loan:** where multiple banks work together to contribute funds in order to provide the required capital. The syndicate of banks share both interest payments from the borrower and risk. Syndicated loans are more viable where the borrower requires a large amount of capital, as these loans can be complicated and expensive to administer.

Borrowers in commercial transactions will typically be companies that own a wide range of assets. Lenders will usually take security over one or more of these assets (as they would over a house when lending to the purchaser of a home). These assets typically include factories, machinery and stock.

However, lenders can take security over a much wider range of assets, for instance: cash the borrower has in its company bank accounts; money the borrower is *owed* but has not yet received from its customers (this money is referred to as 'book debts'); work in progress (i.e. products that have not yet been fully manufactured); the borrower's intellectual property rights; and shares the borrower owns in other companies (e.g. shares in its subsidiaries).

Types Of Security

There are various types of security, for instance 'fixed charges' and 'floating charges'. This section provides a simplified overview of how different types of security (known as 'charges') can operate, although you are unlikely to be expected to discuss the concepts outlined in any real detail in an interview. However, understanding the basic principles can help if you end up interning in a banking/debt finance-related department of a commercial law firm.

> **Mortgage / Fixed Charge:** a fixed charge (or mortgage) gives the lender a legal right to claim and sell the asset(s) over which security is taken (the 'secured assets') in order to recover the funds loaned out, in instances where a loan has not been repaid in accordance with the terms under which the security was taken. The borrower cannot sell the secured assets without the lender's consent, so fixed charges will not usually be suitable for assets such as stock (which companies need to be able to sell to consumers in order to make a profit). Note, mortgages and fixed charges are not identical in all respects. However, discussion of the differences (which relate to the transfer of ownership) is beyond the scope of this handbook.

📖 **Floating Charge:** operates in a similar manner to a fixed charge, but is different in that the assets over which the floating charge is taken *can* be freely sold *unless* the charge 'crystallises'. The parties can agree in advance the circumstances under which the charge will 'crystallise' and these circumstances will usually include the borrower becoming insolvent. This ability to freely sell assets makes floating charges more suitable for assets over which it would commercially impractical for the borrower to relinquish control to the lender (e.g. stock or cash held in a current account). For instance, if a borrower relinquished control of its stock to a lender, that borrower would be unable to sell that stock without receiving permission from the lender to do so each time a customer requested to buy that stock. A floating charge offers less protection for lenders however. This is because lenders that have the benefit of a floating charge are not repaid in the event of insolvency until certain other parties (such as fixed charge holders, the liquidator and unpaid employees) have been repaid in full. This often means that there is little left for floating charge holders after borrowers become insolvent.

📖 **Liquidator:** a party often appointed when a company becomes bankrupt. Functions include: collecting money the (bankrupt) company is owed, collecting and selling that company's assets, then distributing the proceeds to parties that are entitled to receive payment (e.g. existing lenders that have not been fully repaid).

Benefits Of Security

Different types of security can give lenders different degrees of protection, through: (1) enabling lenders to exert differing degrees of control over borrowers; and (2) giving lenders priority over borrowers' assets if those borrowers become insolvent.

Control

- The type of security taken by a lender can dictate the extent to which that lender can *control* the borrower's use of the secured assets.
- For instance, if Lender A takes a 'fixed charge' over Borrower Z's factory, the agreement will likely include terms that prohibit Borrower Z from:
    1. Disposing of (selling) that factory without Lender A's consent; and
    2. Granting security over that factory to other lenders before Lender A has been fully repaid (the clause in an agreement setting out this prohibition is known as a 'negative pledge' clause).
- If instead Borrower Z grants Lender A a 'floating charge' over its assets, Borrower Z will typically remain free to sell the secured assets unless and until certain pre-specified events occur (e.g. Borrower Z fails to make an interest payment to Lender A on time).

📖 **Secured Assets:** assets over which the borrower has granted security to the lender. For example, when a bank lends money to the purchaser of a house, the *house* is typically the 'secured asset'.

Priority

- The type of security taken by a lender can also dictate that lender's ranking in the order of priority.
- If Company A becomes insolvent, its assets will be liquidated (sold off to raise cash) so that the parties to which Company A owes money (Company A's 'creditors') can be repaid. If Company A has borrowed from multiple lenders, all the lenders that are still owed money by Company A will want to be repaid. However, the assets remaining after a borrower becomes insolvent are typically insufficient to repay all the debts it owes. The law deals with such circumstances by setting out a system of priority between lenders.
- Security can ensure that lenders are repaid (out of the proceeds from the sale of the secured assets) in priority to other lenders that either do not have the benefit of security, or have security that ranks lower in priority. The type of security taken by a lender will dictate the extent to which it is given priority over other lenders. Lenders that have fixed charges over a borrower's assets rank above lenders that have floating charges over a borrower's assets, whilst lenders without security over a borrower's assets will generally rank beneath lenders that do have some form of security.
- Note that a company may have possession of property that does not *belong* to it, such as machinery that is leased/borrowed or goods that have been supplied on terms that ensure those goods remain the supplier's property until they have been paid for in full. These items must be returned to their actual owners; they cannot be sold for the benefit of the insolvent company's lenders.

- By way of example, let's assume that Lender A is owed £100,000 and has a fixed charge over Borrower Z's assets; Lender B is owed £100,000 and has a floating charge over Borrower Z's assets; and Lender C is owed £100,000 and has no security over Borrower Z's assets. If Borrower Z becomes insolvent and only £150,000 remains after all its assets have been sold, Lender A will receive back it's £100,000 in full; Lender B will receive back the remaining £50,000 (which covers at least some of the money it is owed); and Lender C will receive back nothing, as unsecured creditors rank lower in the order of priority.

Secured Creditors: lenders that have been granted security over a borrower's assets.

Unsecured Creditors: lenders that do not have the benefit of security over any of a borrower's assets.

- Note that this section provides an oversimplification of the rules governing security. There are other rules that affect the order of priority. Lenders can contractually agree an alternative order of priority between themselves (using 'intercreditor' or 'subordination' agreements), whilst a certain proportion of the assets subject to a floating charge may be set aside ('ring-fenced') for unsecured creditors. Different forms of security may also be better suited to different types of assets. However, for the purposes of this handbook (i.e. interview and internship preparation), the detail in this section should be more than enough.

Issues With Taking Security

Taking security can be an expensive process, as it typically involves the drafting and negotiation of a number of documents and therefore the involvement of a number of financial advisers. Lenders will therefore not usually take security when lending small amounts. Certain types of security may also not be recognised in other jurisdictions (for instance, security involving trustees), but further consideration of this is outside of the scope of this handbook (and is unlikely to be required of you in an interview).

Some corporate borrowers may also be subject to restrictions that prevent them from granting security over their assets to lenders. These restrictions may be in the corporate borrower's constitutional documents (the documents that set out what companies can and cannot do) or in agreements with other lenders (such agreements may include, for instance, a negative pledge clause, as discussed above).

Certain types of security must also be registered. Fixed charges for instance must be registered at Companies House within 21 days starting the day after the security was granted. Failure to register may mean that the security is void, which can have dire consequences for lenders (as they will therefore rank beneath secured creditors in the order of priority and may thus not receive back any of the money they are owed).

nsolvency

As mentioned earlier, a company is 'insolvent' when it cannot pay its debts in time, or when the total of its liabilities exceeds its assets. If a company becomes insolvent, it must cease trading. There are various arrangements that can be put in place to try to avoid a company becoming insolvent. These arrangements may be initiated by a company's directors or creditors and involve placing differing levels of external control upon the company's operations.

The arrangement(s) chosen will depend on the aims of a company, the extent of its financial difficulties and the intentions of its creditors. A brief overview of potential arrangements has been provided below, although any in-depth consideration of this topic is beyond the scope of this handbook:

- **Loans/Raising Additional Finance:** directors could renegotiate the terms of existing loans with creditors in order to give the company more time to repay those loans. The company should, where possible, avoid taking on additional debt as this could make the company less financially stable. Issuing new shares could provide a more viable source of additional finance, if demand for the company's shares still exists (which may be unlikely).
- **Profitability/Cash Flow:** every effort should be made to improve profitability, including cost cutting and undertaking regular and thorough reviews of the company's business plan/objectives/accounts. Directors should try to improve cash flow, perhaps by trying to extend credit periods with existing suppliers or finding cheaper alternative suppliers. Customer debts could also be collected more effectively and dividend payments should be temporarily suspended.
- **Turnaround Specialists:** directors could also consider consulting with turnaround specialists (who are responsible for helping companies to recover from financial difficulties).

However, if a company *is* insolvent or there is *no reasonable prospect* that it can avoid becoming insolvent, the directors must cease trading or could face legal action (e.g. a claim for 'wrongful trading').

Starting, Running & Growing A Business

Starting, running or growing a business can require the acquisition and utilisation of a wide range of resources and capabilities and typically involves a huge degree of risk. Consequently, the reality is that many new businesses fail.

Strategic Challenges

Barriers to entry may reduce the chances of a business successfully starting up or entering a new market. Such barriers include: financial barriers; complicated or restrictive regulation (for instance certain jurisdictions may not allow foreign businesses to enter particular local markets); an inability to compete against established competitors; various risks and uncertainties; and a lack of resources.

Costs

- The primary aim of most businesses is to generate profit. To do this, a business' revenue (turnover) must exceed its fixed costs and variable costs. Profits increase as costs decrease or revenue increases. Therefore, keeping costs as low as possible is essential if a business is to maximise its profit margins.

📖 **Profit Margin:** the amount of profit generated per item after deducting the average cost of producing each item.

📖 **Revenue / Turnover / Sales:** the total income generated from a firm's operations within a period of time. This does not take into account costs, instead purely reflecting the money that has been received from consumer sales. For example, if a company sells 10 handbooks for £8 each, its revenue would be £80.

📖 **Fixed Costs:** business costs that remain the same regardless of the number of units produced or sold. Examples include: the rent paid for an office or a factory; the cost of paying utility bills; or the cost of fuel for an aeroplane flight. These costs will all remain the same (or almost the same) regardless of whether a company sells 0 or 1000 units.

📖 **Variable Costs:** costs that change in relation to the number of units produced or sold, for instance the cost of packaging or delivering each individual product. Labour to some extent is a variable cost as over time, the number of employees may change to reflect a company's level of output. However, in the short term, labour is generally a fixed cost.

- There are various strategies that businesses can employ to minimise or stabilise costs. For instance: maximising economies of scale; integrating into the supply chain; outsourcing; offshoring; entering long-term contracts; and utilising derivatives.

📖 **Economies Of Scale:** the cost advantage gained as output increases. This cost advantage arises when fixed costs are spread across a greater quantity of sales. When organisations place larger orders with suppliers, suppliers will usually pass on a proportion of the cost savings they receive through economies of scale to that firm, in turn reducing that firm's input costs.

📖 **Integrate Into The Supply Chain:** the supply chain is comprised of contributors involved in the process leading up to the sale of a product (e.g. manufacturers). Typically, each contributor will charge prices that include a profit margin. If one company takes control of two or more stages in the supply chain, it will not have to pay this additional margin and costs will consequently decrease.

📖 **Outsourcing:** contracting out various roles or processes to external companies, for instance customer services, distribution, or marketing. Businesses can benefit in numerous ways, for example through outsourcing to parties with greater expertise or experience in undertaking a particular role; or through the flexibility outsourcing may enable. For instance, if demand for a firm's products or services decreases, it must still pay employee wages (at least in the short term). However, if a firm outsources its labour requirements (i.e. pays another company to provide employees as and when they are required) and demand subsequently decreases, the firm can simply end its contract with the company that provided the employees. This would enable the firm to consequently avoid paying for employees that are no longer needed (subject to the terms of the outsourcing agreement).

📖 **Offshoring:** shifting elements of production or distribution abroad, usually to countries in which costs (e.g. labour) are lower.

📖 **Long-Term Contracts:** these can enable companies to more accurately predict future costs, or to mitigate the risk of price increases if, for instance, the price of raw materials increases globally. Participants in the supply chain may also provide more favourable rates to businesses willing to commit to long-term relationships.

📖 **Derivatives:** financial contracts relating to underlying assets (such as securities or commodities). Examples include futures, which are agreements between parties to engage in a transaction on a predetermined future date at a specified price; and options, which give one party the right (but do not obligate them) to purchase or sell a product on a predetermined future date at a specified price. These derivatives can help companies to better predict future costs and mitigate the risk of adverse price movements reducing profitability (this is known as hedging risk). This can in turn facilitate more accurate financial planning.

📖 **Securities:** financing and investment instruments such as bonds and shares.

To learn about the Profitability Framework and how to apply it in case study interviews, check out:

www.CityCareerSeries.com → Applications & Interviews → Case Study Interviews

Competition / Saturated Market

- If there are existing competitors in the market that are more established it may be difficult for new businesses to compete. Established businesses may benefit from having recognisable brands and trusted relationships with consumers. The consequent customer loyalty may prevent customers from switching to a product offered by a new market entrant.

- Established businesses are also more likely to receive preferential rates from supply chain participants such as suppliers, reducing costs to a level that new businesses would struggle to match (having had little or no opportunity to earn good will or trust). In addition, an established business may benefit from economies of scale, enabling superior cost control and wider profit margins than that which a new entrant may be able to attain. Consequently, established firms may be able to undercut prices charged by new entrants.

- To compete in saturated markets (meaning markets with many competitors), new firms may thus require a unique selling point. Firms could offer a product or service with unique attributes that differentiate that product or service from competitors', or find a way to significantly undercut competitor prices (as Ryanair did in the airline industry). Such unique selling points could provide new entrants with a competitive advantage, resulting in a greater chance of success.

Uncertainty

- If businesses produce new products, uncertainties arise as to whether there will be sufficient demand for those products to generate profit. Conducting extensive market research before fully investing in the design, production, distribution and marketing of products can mitigate this risk, enabling businesses to modify and adapt offerings to suit consumer preferences.

Resources / Capabilities

- Does the company have human resources with the necessary capabilities (skills, experience and expertise) to create, brand, distribute and market a viable product or service? Does the business have the necessary physical resources to successfully operate, most notably start-up capital, cash for operations, machinery and offices?

- A business lacking the necessary capabilities and resources could consider partnering with other businesses or employing people who have: relevant business experience, a network of beneficial contacts (which could facilitate the financing, production and distribution processes), knowledge of the target market, or the resources required to effectively operate. For example, small businesses could share resources such as office space, whilst start-ups could partner with individual investors willing to provide capital and other relevant resources in exchange for equity. Such investors are typically known as business angels.

Why Acquire, Merge With Or Cooperate With A Business?

Businesses acquire, merge with or cooperate with other businesses for a variety of reasons, many of which relate to the synergies that can arise. However, a less permanent solution may be to engage in alliances, partnerships or joint ventures, which give rise to similar benefits but also enable parties to retain some autonomy.

Acquisition: when one business purchases another, either through mutual consent or through a hostile takeover.

Merger: when multiple businesses voluntarily and permanently combine to form one business.

Alliance / Partnership: when businesses or individuals with complementary capabilities/resources cooperate in order to advance their mutual interests. For example, the inventor of a product may engage in a partnership with a lawyer, distributor or marketing agency. The parties typically share the costs, risks and rewards.

Joint Venture: when two or more businesses agree to pool their resources and work together on a specific task or project, such as the development or launch of a product. The parties typically share the costs, risks and rewards.

Synergies: synergies refer to the benefits that can result from the interaction between two companies. Examples of synergies include: the sharing of resources to reduce costs and the sharing of knowledge/human resources to improve product offerings. Synergies can ensure that the value generated by companies that have been combined exceeds the overall value that those companies could produce separately.

Below are some of the advantages of acquiring/merging with/cooperating with other companies:

✓ **Access To New Markets And Customers:** this should facilitate an increase in sales.

✓ **Access To Complementary Resources:** organisations can boost their own capabilities. For instance other businesses or partners may possess physical, financial or technical resources, expertise (market specific knowledge), complementary skills, supply chain relationships (for instance access to suppliers and distributors), or networks and contacts that enable firms to circumvent barriers to entry and compete more effectively.

✓ **Economies Of Scope:** firms may benefit from collaborations that will enable them to diversify their product range. Selling a greater range of products could attract new customers and consequently increase sales. Bundling products with those of complementary businesses (for instance a mobile phone manufacturer linking with an Internet service provider or mobile game creator) could also improve a businesses' product offering.

✓ **Efficiency:** if organisations combine and enlarge their operations, this could enable them to buy, produce and sell in greater quantities, consequently giving rise to increased economies of scale and thus lower costs. Integrating into the supply chain (by acquiring or partnering with supply chain actors) could reduce external costs. In addition, combining knowledge, expertise and resources could enable firms to increase operational efficiency and thus reduce internal costs.

✓ **Savings:** companies could share costs such as infrastructure rent, marketing or research and development.

✓ **Reputation:** organisations may influence others' perceptions of their capabilities through gaining external legitimacy, which can in turn increase trust from suppliers, lenders and customers. Linking with an established organisation in a new market (for instance Tesco partnering with Tata in India) may reduce consumer suspicion, encouraging consumers to make purchases.

✓ **Innovation:** increasing access to resources and capabilities may foster innovation.

✓ **Competition:** forming alliances with, merging with, or acquiring other businesses reduces direct competition in the market. This can increase a firm's market power, which lessens its need to reduce prices in order to compete.

There are however issues that can arise when businesses combine/cooperate:

✗ **Loss Of Control / Conflict:** profits and decisions may have to be shared. Reaching an efficient consensus on decisions may be difficult if the motives or objectives of the parties involved do not align.

✗ **Administration / Costs:** coordinating and integrating different businesses can be a complex and costly process.

✗ **Inefficiency:** communication issues may arise if an organisation becomes more complex. In addition, multiple alliances with similar partners may yield fewer benefits than partnerships with differentiated partners.

✗ **Expropriation:** a larger, more powerful company may steal customers, expertise, assets or processes and then terminate the agreement. Ensuring intellectual property rights are sufficiently protected can mitigate this risk.

How To Grow A Business

Businesses can achieve growth organically; through acquiring or merging with other businesses; through expanding into other markets (e.g. countries); or through engaging in an alliance with one or more other businesses.

Organic Growth

Growth facilitated by an increase in demand achieved, for instance, through effective marketing and branding, expanding distribution (perhaps through exporting), diversifying the product range, licensing or franchising. Below are some of the advantages and disadvantages of growing a business organically.

- ✓ **Reduced Risk:** there is generally less risk in the sense that growth depends more on a natural increase in demand, rather than estimates and projections of the potential returns that an acquisition could generate.
- ✓ **Easier Integration:** easier for a firm to retain its culture, protect its brand and maintain effective communication.
- ✗ **Slow Expansion:** growth may be slower than growth achieved through acquiring other organisations.
- ✗ **Costs:** it can be expensive to build brands from scratch in new jurisdictions, as this can require extensive market research and large-scale promotional campaigns.
- ✗ **Increased Risk:** Foreign Direct Investment (FDI), for instance opening a new store abroad, is risky as it can be difficult to break into new markets if more established competitors exist. In contrast, exporting or franchising can be less risky alternatives, as these do not require direct investment (such as purchasing a factory or an office building abroad).

📖 **Exporting:** when firms sell products from their home country to other countries. It can enable firms to expand their operations without committing to direct investment in another country, thus reducing risk and costs. However, distribution (e.g. transportation) costs, currency value fluctuations and potentially high taxes may hinder effective cost control.

📖 **Franchising:** when firms sell the right for others to set up identical firms under the same name (using the same brand and selling the same products) in exchange for a lump sum payment and/or royalties. This can enable rapid expansion that boosts a franchisor's brand exposure and customer base. A franchisor can usually exert some control over a franchisee to ensure that the franchisee does not act in a manner that damages the brand. Starbucks and Burger King are good examples of franchises.

📖 **Licensing:** when one firm permits another firm to use an element of its business, for instance the right to manufacture its products, incorporate its technology into a product or use its intellectual property (IP) rights, usually in exchange for a royalty. If a firm lacks the capabilities to commercialise a product but has developed the technology, licensing to a firm that can commercialise it could provide a source of revenue. However, if the technology is embedded into a product, the licensor may generate little brand recognition or customer loyalty. There is also a risk that the licensee will expropriate the technology and emerge as a competitor.

Acquisitive / Equity-Based Growth

Growth achieved through acquiring, merging with or working with other companies. This can involve sharing profits and risk. Below are some of the advantages and disadvantages of acquisitive/equity-based growth.

- ✓ **Rapid Expansion:** can facilitate rapid expansion through providing immediate access to, for instance, distribution networks, customers, employees, or retail outlets that are under the control of another firm.
- ✓ **Additional Experience:** one firm can benefit from the experience that another firm may have accumulated in new markets. This can help it to learn about new markets quickly, reducing the costs associated with market research and increasing its chances of commercial success.
- ✗ **Costs:** it can be very costly to purchase other firms, as payment of a premium for the target company's shares (payment of a higher price than the market value) and extensive fees to legal/financial advisors may be required.
- ✗ **Time:** it can be very time consuming to purchase other firms, as ample negotiation and shareholder consent may be required.
- ✗ **Complexity:** effective integration can be difficult to achieve if the organisations involved are large and complex.

How To Value A Business

Debt + Equity

- Add together the value of a business' equity (capital, assets etc.) then subtract the value of its liabilities (debt).

Discounted Cash Flow (DCF)

- DCF analysis can be used to value a company or project. Complex calculations are used to estimate the returns (cash) that would be received over time as a result of purchasing the target business. The figure is 'discounted' or 'adjusted' to take into account the changing value of money over time. The sum of all future cash flows (in and out) is known as the net present value (NPV). This can help to project the potential value a proposed investment could generate.

Return On Capital Employed (ROCE)

- Investors may take into account any financial returns previously received by investors (for example the size of dividends paid out or the growth rate of share prices) in addition to future projections of investor returns.

Combined Value

- An investor could consider the additional value a target company could bring to their existing business. Does the target business complement their existing business in a manner that could increase the overall value of the newly combined company post-combination? Could a merger help an investor to reduce costs (through enabling greater economies of scale or boosting their bargaining power with suppliers); acquire complementary skill sets and expertise; reduce competition; or increase their overall influence in the market? If so, an investor may be willing to pay a premium in order to acquire another business.

> 🕮 **Premium:** paying a premium means paying an amount that exceeds the market value of a product or company. Premiums can be offered by potential purchasers (or borrowers) to persuade sellers (or lenders) to engage in transactions. Buyers will offer premiums in the belief that they will be able to extract additional value from the target company post-acquisition, either because it is under-valued, underperforming or unable to operate as efficiently as it could if controlled by the buyer.

Intangible Resources

- Investors could consider whether the target business has formed political, social or commercial relationships that could be beneficial. Take into account the value of human capital. For instance, does the business have a unique management team that affords it a competitive advantage?

Comparable Analysis / Precedent Transactions

- Investors would likely also take into account the prices that have been paid for similar businesses under similar circumstances.

Earnings Before Interest, Tax, Depreciation & Amortisation (EBITDA) Multiple

- When valuing Company A, investors may start by looking at the enterprise value (EV), meaning the market value, of a similar company, for example Company B. They will divide Company B's enterprise value by its EBITDA to give its EV/EBITDA multiple; then multiply Company A's EBITDA by Company B's EV/EBITDA multiple to estimate the enterprise value of Company A. For instance, if Company B's enterprise value is £1million and its EBITDA is £100,000, its EBITDA multiple would be 10. If Company A's EBITDA is £50,000, this would then be multiplied by 10 to give an estimated enterprise value of £500,000.

- Excluding interest, tax, depreciation and amortisation from calculations makes it easier to compare two similar companies on a like-for-like basis, giving investors a better indication of which company is more inherently profitable. This is because interest and tax payments may depend on a company's capital structure or location, whilst depreciation and amortisation figures can be subjective and thus do not necessarily reflect a company's potential to generate profit in the future.

📖 **Depreciation:** refers to the decrease in value of tangible (physical) assets over time. An older asset that has been regularly used is going to be worth less than a newer version of the same asset, as it is more likely to break or work with reduced efficiency.

📖 **Amortisation:** refers (in this context) to the decrease in value of intangible assets over time. For example, a patent may decrease in value as its expiry date approaches.

Future Potential Of The Business

- Investors could consider the overall prospects of the market in which a business operates and whether any opportunities are likely to arise that will boost profitability. For instance, if a sports equipment chain in London is the subject of a valuation and investors are aware that the Olympics are set to commence in the near future, they may be willing to pay a greater amount for the business in the knowledge that sales are likely to significantly increase during and after the Olympics. Growth projections for similar products, businesses and industries may also be taken into account.

- In addition, Investors could consider where a target business' products are at in the product life cycle. Do the products have the potential to sell at a similar rate to that which has generated current profitability levels, or will sales likely diminish? For instance, if a patent belonging to the target business is about to expire, competitors may be able to subsequently copy and sell the technology themselves, attracting customers away from the target business.

📖 **Product Life Cycle:** the period over which a product enters and eventually exits the market. The number of sales typically increases after a product is released and initially marketed. The number of sales then tends to stabilise and eventually diminish as more competitors enter the market and the product is replaced by cheaper or superior alternatives.

We have produced some additional resources to help you structure your analysis of problems in case study interviews. These can be found at:

www.CityCareerSeries.com → Applications & Interviews → Case Study Interviews

Anatomy Of An Acquisition

The Process

Stage 1: Pitch

- Law firms must pitch to clients in order to be selected as their legal advisor (or one of their legal advisors) for a transaction (or a set period). Pitches usually focus on the firm's capabilities, experience and the ways in which it can offer value for money.

Stage 2: Internal / External Checks

- Law firms must check they are not engaging in work on any projects or for any clients that may give rise to a conflict of interest.
- Law firms must thoroughly research clients to ensure they have not engaged in illegal activities such as money laundering.

Stage 3: Initial Instructions

- The primary objectives of the client must be ascertained.
- An appropriate fee structure and approximate timetable for the execution of the proposed transaction must be established.

Stage 4: Resourcing

- Managing transactions can involve coordinating different practice areas internally to source the required specialist advice for different elements of the transaction, whilst also coordinating external parties involved. Lawyers must help to determine which offices, teams, key employees and external parties will be required to execute the transaction.

Stage 5: Offer Process

- Clients may require protection throughout the bid (offer) process, for instance exclusivity for a set period.

> **Exclusivity Agreement / Lockout Clause:** buyers may request exclusivity over a proposed transaction for a period of time so that they do not waste time and money undertaking due diligence and negotiating only to lose out to another party.

Stage 6: Buyer Protection (see below)

Stage 7: Deal Execution (structuring and financing the transaction - see below)

Other Parties Involved

Sellers (sometimes referred to as 'vendors') / Buyers (buyers are also typically borrowers)

- For instance, private individuals (including directors), investors (including shareholders, business angels, private equity firms, venture capital firms and institutional investors), corporations and public bodies.

> 🕮 **Business Angels:** business angels (or "angel investors") are wealthy individuals who invest their personal income in early-stage businesses in exchange for equity. Working with a business angel can be especially beneficial for a business if that business angel has ample knowledge of, and experience working in, that business' industry.

> 🕮 **Private Equity Firms / Venture Capital Firms:** these aggregate funds from institutional investors and private individuals. They aim to buy businesses at low prices (typically because the businesses are underperforming or undervalued), cut costs, improve efficiency and then subsequently sell at a profit.

> 🕮 **Institutional Investors:** institutions with specialist knowledge that trade securities (such as shares) in large quantities, usually on behalf of others. Examples include pension funds, insurance companies, investment banks and hedge funds.

Lenders

- For instance, private investors, banks, private equity firms and institutional investors seeking a return on their capital. These will typically base a decision to lend on the potential level of return and the borrower's credit rating, reputation and performance.

Investment Banks

- Financial advisors that typically advise and assist corporations and public bodies looking to raise money. This includes linking clients to potential investors; facilitating the issue of shares or bonds, for instance through helping to price the issue; and analysing the financial state of companies for the purpose of valuation and risk analysis. Investment banks also trade securities such as bonds, shares and derivatives on behalf of clients.

Accountants / Auditors

- Help to prepare or verify financial statements and analyse the financial state of companies for the purpose of valuation and risk analysis.

Consultants

- Advise on existing strategies, firm performance and potential future strategies.

Public Relations

- Can be enlisted to promote the fact that the parties are acting appropriately, thus minimising negative public attention.

Regulatory Bodies

- Set and enforce various legal requirements with which parties must comply when executing transactions. Notable examples include the Financial Conduct Authority (FCA) and the Competition department of the European Commission.

Environmental / Social Impact Experts

- Assess the environmental or social implications of transactions to help determine whether legal implications could arise.

Companies House

- Incorporated companies must be registered with Companies House and must (under the Companies Act 2006) file information including annual accounts and returns. Companies House must also be notified if certain changes are made to companies.

Buyer Protection

Without adequate protection, buyers may be left with unexpected liabilities or without a remedy if, after the deal is completed, it transpires that the agreements made or expectations generated prior to completion have not been upheld. There are numerous ways in which lawyers can help clients mitigate this risk, such as seeking competition clearance in advance, conducting thorough due diligence and ensuring various contractual provisions are in place in favour of the buyer, including warranties and indemnities.

Competition Law

Clearance must usually be secured from the relevant competition authorities (such as the European Commission) for proposed mergers or acquisitions. If the proposed transaction could significantly reduce competition in the market (for instance through creating a monopoly) the transaction may be deemed anti-competitive in accordance with various regulations. Consequently, the transaction may be prohibited; the acquirer may receive a substantial fine; or the transaction may be allowed to continue if certain terms are met, for instance terms requiring the buyer to sell part of their existing business (or part of the target post-acquisition).

Due Diligence

📖 **Due Diligence:** refers to the process under which a potential buyer and its advisors carry out an in-depth investigation into many aspects of a target company, in order to gain a solid understanding of that company's business and/or market. Due diligence can help a potential buyer to decide whether to go ahead with the purchase and if so, at what price and on which terms. "Vendor due diligence" refers to the process under which a seller and its advisers carry out an in-depth investigation into the company (or group of companies) that the seller is intending to sell. This can enable the seller (at an early stage) to identify and rectify any issues that consequently come to light, which can reduce the risk of potential buyers walking away from the deal or demanding a reduction in price.

When conducting due diligence, companies (or their lawyers) are usually given access to a 'data room' (nowadays this is typically an online database) containing comprehensive information relevant to the transaction including: commercial contracts, financial records and information on existing assets and liabilities. This helps bidders to understand in greater detail that which they are considering purchasing and provides advisers with an opportunity to discover (and subsequently mitigate) any potential issues.

Sellers may put restrictions in place to prevent potential buyers (which may well also be existing competitors) from discovering too much about the company, thus reducing the ability of potential buyers to use such information to their own advantage if the deal falls through at a later stage. A confidentiality agreement could mitigate this risk.

📖 **Confidentiality Agreement / Non-Disclosure Agreement (NDA):** sellers can deter potential buyers from publicly revealing sensitive information that those potential buyers receive during the due diligence process by ensuring that they sign confidentiality agreements. This can ensure companies (which may also be competitors) do not benefit from inside knowledge relating to the seller's company if the proposed transaction falls through.

Assets

- Acquisitions will typically involve the transfer of tangible assets such as inventory, machinery, buildings and vehicles and intangible assets such as shares and intellectual property rights. Due diligence can help ascertain which assets are actually included in a deal; whether the seller has the legal right to sell the assets in question; whether assets are subject to any charges or restrictions (for instance a mortgage or a right of usage granted to a third party such as an easement); and whether assets are in a satisfactory condition.

📖 **Liquidity:** how easily a business' assets can be converted into cash. If a company is highly liquid, it can easily convert its assets into cash. This may be important if a bidder plans to sell some of the target's assets post-transaction.

Contracts

- Lawyers must check whether key actors in the supply chain such as employees, suppliers, distributors and customers have change of control clauses in their contracts. If such actors are able to terminate their contract with the company in the event of a takeover, this may reduce the buyer's ability to operate effectively post-acquisition. If such clauses exist, purchasers must assess whether these actors are key to the success of the business and consider whether these actors may attempt to leverage a new owner's dependency on their offerings to secure more favourable contractual terms or simply refuse to uphold existing contracts in any form.

- If this is likely to be the case, purchasers (or their lawyers) could consider whether viable alternatives exist that may reduce the bargaining power of existing actors, or whether negotiations with these actors should take place before a purchaser commits to an acquisition.

Change Of Control Clause / Break Clause: such clauses can enable parties that are contracted to work with a company to terminate the contract without incurring any liability for breach of contract if control of the company changes hands.

- Lawyers may consider devising ways in which to incentivise those involved with the company to remain so, for instance through offering existing actors in the supply chain long-term contracts, or providing key employees with share options, pay rises, or guarantees relating to the security of their employment. This is advice typically given by lawyers in the Employment (or Benefits) departments of law firms.
- Buyers may also require sellers to sign non-solicit clauses to mitigate the risk of sellers luring certain key contributors (e.g. employees or suppliers) away from the company post-acquisition.

Non-Solicit Clause: a contractual promise from a seller to a buyer not to approach and attempt to poach, for instance, certain key employees, suppliers, distributors or customers of the newly purchased company for a given time period or in a particular jurisdiction.

Liabilities

Unless the contrary is agreed, once firms have been acquired, the new purchasers assume responsibility for any existing liabilities of the acquired company. Due diligence must thus be conducted before a sale to ensure that there are no outstanding liabilities of which a potential purchaser is unaware, as such liabilities could significantly reduce the value of the transaction. It is essential that the purchaser is made aware of such liabilities, as this may influence their decision to buy and the price they are willing to pay.

- **Debt:** includes outstanding loans, unpaid overdrafts, payments owed to suppliers, distributors or customers and bonds that have been issued and have not yet matured (meaning that the company must continue to make coupon payments to bondholders). A purchaser could require a warranty that no undisclosed debt exists.
- **Outstanding Litigation:** if pending litigation is settled post-acquisition, the purchaser will be liable to pay any damages awarded. It is thus essential for the purchaser to secure an indemnity for the seller against any such costs that may later arise and/or an undertaking that the litigation will be settled before the acquisition is completed. This could also cover any litigation that is not pending, but arises in the future as a result of the target's activities pre-acquisition.
- **Pension Scheme Liability:** purchasers will be liable for future pension payments that a company is obligated to make, including payments that accrued as a result of work carried out pre-acquisition. Lawyers must thus check whether a target has enough capital set aside to fulfil these liabilities and could request a warranty regarding the state of a company's pension scheme.

Warranties: statements of existing fact in contracts. These amount to assurances or promises relating to the present condition of an object or entity, the breach of which may give rise to a legal claim for damages. For instance, a seller may provide a warranty (to a buyer) that it is not currently involved in any litigation.

Undertakings: statements, given orally or in writing, promising to take/refrain from taking certain action in the future. The statements must be given in the course of business/legal practice by someone held out as representing the firm (i.e. including secretaries and trainees), to a party that reasonably places reliance on them. For instance, a seller may undertake (to a buyer) that it will settle any pending litigation before completion of an acquisition and to reduce the purchase price by any amount it pays out as part of that settlement agreement. It does not matter whether the undertaking explicitly includes the word 'undertake', although statements of intention do not constitute undertakings.

Indemnities: promises to pay the other party pound for pound compensation if specified scenarios take place. For instance, if the target company is in the middle of a law suit at the time it is acquired, the seller can agree to reimburse the buyers in the future for any money that the target company is required to pay out in relation to the law suit once it comes under the buyer's control. Indemnities may be subject to financial caps, i.e. limits on the amount that the seller will have to pay out if a claim relating to the circumstances covered by the indemnity is made. Indemnities may also be subject to time limitations, meaning that after a pre-agreed period of time post-acquisition, the buyer can no longer rely upon the indemnities.

Other Contractual Protections

There are various other contractual protections available that can pre-empt and mitigate, or help to determine the outcome of, potential issues that could arise post-acquisition. Notable examples include non-compete and entire agreement clauses.

Non-Compete Agreement: a promise from the seller that if the deal goes ahead, the seller will not start up a similar business and emerge as a competitor of the business being acquired. Such agreements will usually apply for a limited period of time (typically 3 years) and/or apply only to regions in which the business being acquired already operates.

Entire Agreement Clause: clause stating that only the terms contained within the contract apply to the agreement and thus any previous negotiations or oral statements that are not recorded in the contract do not apply or bind the parties.

The parties to a transaction will also usually subject the Sale and Purchase Agreement to conditions precedent.

Conditions Precedent: conditions that must be fulfilled before full performance under a contract becomes due. Notable examples of conditions precedent include the verification (through due diligence) of all the key promises made by the seller prior to the transaction and the receipt of clearance from the relevant competition authorities.

How To Purchase A Business (Structuring A Transaction)

When deciding how to purchase a business, buyers must consider whether a share or an asset purchase best suits their needs. Below are some of the advantages and disadvantages of different methods of purchasing a business.

Share Sale/Purchase: this involves a purchaser buying either all of another company's shares, or a controlling stake in another company. Following a share sale, the target company retains all its assets and liabilities; the purchaser simply acquires the target company's *shares.* The purchaser will however *indirectly* own/take on the target's assets/liabilities by virtue of its ownership of the target's shares.

- ✓ **Control:** easier for purchasers to gain full control over a company, including its human capital, tangible assets (e.g. plant and machinery) and intangible assets (e.g. business relationships, good will/brand loyalty, intellectual property rights, and knowledge of internal processes).
- ✓ **Savings:** purchasers are exempt from goods and services tax if acquiring assets through a share sale.
- ✗ **Shareholders:** it may be difficult for purchasers to persuade a sufficient proportion of shareholders to agree to a sale.
- ✗ **Risk:** purchasers will take on sellers' existing liabilities and obligations.

Asset Sale/Purchase: this involves a purchaser buying specific assets owned by another company, such as buildings or patents.

- ✓ **Flexibility:** the flexibility to acquire only the assets that compliment a purchaser's existing business can result in a transaction that is more financially efficient.
- ✓ **Valuation:** valuation may be less subjective as intangible assets such as customer loyalty need not be considered.
- ✓ **Due Diligence:** due diligence relating to specific assets may be quicker and easier to conduct than firm-wide investigations.
- ✓ **Risk:** it is less risky in the sense that a purchaser has a lower risk of taking on unforeseen liabilities.
- ✓ **Tax:** tax law in the UK enables the market value of assets purchased to be offset against tax, even if the purchaser paid less than the market value.
- ✗ **Control:** purchasers will not gain full control over the entire company and may thus fail to benefit from any employees or internal knowledge and processes that may have helped to facilitate efficient and effective utilisation of the assets.

Financing A Deal

In its early stages, a business may take out small loans, apply for government grants, or receive investment from venture capital firms/business angels. As a business grows and matures, it may use its cash resources to fund day-to-day operations and increasingly use debt (where the investors are lenders) or issuances of equity (where the investors become part-owners). Large businesses may combine multiple forms of financing, for instance issuing shares (equity) whilst also taking on multiple layers of debt from different sources (for instance taking loans or issuing bonds).

Note that businesses may borrow money even if they have cash available. For instance, a business may choose to invest available cash in a new venture and borrow money to fund day-to-day operations (or use available cash to fund day-to-day operations and use money borrowed to invest in a new venture) in the hope that the profits generated by that new venture will exceed the cost of borrowing money to use in place of the available cash.

If a business becomes insolvent, the ways in which the repayment of different creditors is organised and prioritised can depend on the type of financing they have provided (debt or equity) and the nature of the contractual agreements made between the parties. The repayment of senior debt holders is prioritised over the repayment of other creditors if a company becomes insolvent. They generally receive lower interest payments, as they are more likely to be repaid and often take security over a company's assets. Junior (subordinated) debt holders are ranked below senior debt holders and therefore will only be repaid once senior creditors have been repaid in full (if any money remains). Subordinated creditors may charge more interest to compensate for this additional risk.

Below are some of the most common methods businesses use to finance deals.

Cash Reserves: financing operations using existing cash resources (for instance, retained profit).

- ✓ **Control:** the owners retain full ownership and control of the business and its assets.
- ✓ **Cost Savings:** no interest payments or dividends will need to be paid.
- ✓ **Arranging Finance:** businesses can access their own capital immediately and without incurring hefty administration fees.
- ✗ **Effectiveness:** some firms may not have enough cash to finance investment and maintain sufficient cash flow.

Bank Loan / Overdraft: firms can borrow from banks and then pay back the loans in instalments, plus interest. The interest rate can be fixed (making it easier for a business to predict its costs) or floating, in which case the rate may be linked to the fluctuation of a benchmark interest rate (for instance LIBOR), which could in turn end up costing less than fixed rate repayments if interest rates happen to fall. A bank may be persuaded to issue a loan on the strength of a well-prepared business plan, a strong previous relationship with the borrower, a financial guarantee from another party, or a company's ability to provide collateral.

- ✓ **Control:** the owners generally retain full ownership and control of the business so long as repayments are met. Note however that lenders may be able to exert some control over a borrower's business through taking security over assets on terms that restrict the ability of the borrower to sell those assets.
- ✓ **Cost Savings:** money can be borrowed as and when it is required, meaning that the borrower may only have to make interest payments that reflect the actual capital in use (i.e. the money drawn out of the bank account). In addition, interest payments made are tax deductible.
- ✓ **Effectiveness:** banks are generally more suited to complicated lending structures as they have extensive experience of evaluating risk. They may thus be more inclined to approve financing and once a loan is approved, a business is generally guaranteed to receive the full amount immediately. Banks may however decide to hedge risk through releasing funds in instalments. This could prevent borrowers from using capital recklessly or for purposes not previously agreed. Under such circumstances, borrowers may only qualify for new instalments once certain targets have been met.
- ✓ **Arranging Finance:** small loans are quicker and cheaper to arrange than bond or share issues. However, as mentioned, large, syndicated loans may be incredibly costly and complicated to arrange.
- ✗ **Security**: collateral may be required in return for a loan, typically in the form of an asset. If repayments are not met, lenders may seize and sell any secured assets in order to retrieve their money. In addition, companies lacking valuable assets may struggle to secure loans due to their inability to offer sufficient collateral.
- ✗ **Costs:** interest payments may be substantial, depending on a borrower's credit rating and the state of the economy.
- ✗ **Repayable On Demand:** certain loans (notably overdrafts) are repayable on demand, which could cause cash-flow issues if repayment is demanded earlier than expected.

📖 **Capital Markets:** these are financial markets that link organisations seeking capital and investors looking to supply capital. Securities including shares and bonds are traded in the capital markets between governments and companies seeking capital, banks, private investors and other investors such as hedge funds and pension funds.

📖 **Bond Issue:** this is where a company (the 'issuer') sells bonds (similar to IOUs) through the debt capital markets. Bonds are purchased by investors and entitle them to a periodic interest payment (coupon) in addition to a lump sum repayment of the principal amount after a set period (when the bond 'matures').

✓ **Control:** bond issuers do not have to offer bond purchasers security over their assets (meaning issuers remain free to use their assets as they see fit) and bondholders rarely try to restrict a bond issuer's business operations.

✓ **Effectiveness:** access to multiple investors through the capital markets makes it easier to raise large amounts.

✗ **Demand:** if a company has a low credit rating or a low profile, it may struggle to sell enough bonds to raise all the capital it requires (and banks may be unwilling to underwrite the issue). To stimulate demand, companies sometimes offer bonds with higher returns (known as 'high yield' or 'junk' bonds).

✗ **Arranging Finance:** bond issues are expensive to arrange, as many terms need to be set out. A bond issue is therefore unsuitable for companies raising only a small amount of capital.

📖 **Underwriters:** bond issues involve underwriters (investment banks) which typically agree (for a fee) to purchase all the bonds in advance and then sell them on to investors, or to purchase any unsold bonds post-issuance.

📖 **Prospectus:** legally required document that must precede bond or share issues. It advertises the issue to potential investors and contains information about the issuer's business, the potential risks and the issuing firm's financial circumstances in addition to the terms and conditions of the issue.

📖 **Share Issue:** this is where a company sells ('issues') its shares. Investors provide money in exchange for shares that represent an ownership stake in a company, with the aim of reaping returns in the form of capital growth (if those shares are later sold at a profit) and dividends (if the company elects to pay dividends).

📖 **Initial Public Offering (IPO):** this is where a company lists its shares on a stock exchange for the *first* time (hence the phrase *initial* public offering) in order to sell those shares through the equity capital markets. Listing through a stock exchange also facilitates the subsequent trading of those shares.

📖 **Business angels:** business angels (or "angel investors") are wealthy individuals who invest their personal income in early-stage businesses in exchange for equity. Working with a business angel can be especially beneficial for a business if that business angel has ample knowledge of, and experience working in, that business' industry.

In general, the advantages and disadvantages of equity investments can include:

✓ **Cost Savings:** no interest payments are required, thus preserving cash flow. In addition, if the company goes bankrupt, the loss is spread across all shareholders.

✓ **No Security:** no security is required, meaning a company will not risk having its assets seized as a result of it issuing shares and subsequently failing to generate sufficient profit.

✓ **Complementary Skills:** some investors (e.g. business angels and private equity firms) may contribute skills, experience, expertise and contacts that benefit the company.

✓ **Profile:** listing on a stock exchange can enhance a company's profile. This can increase its access to the market for capital and enable it to negotiate more preferential terms with suppliers and creditors.

✗ **Control:** equity represents a stake of ownership and thus control among existing owners is diluted as additional shareholders join. Shareholders are afforded certain rights including the right to vote and significant company decisions may be subject to shareholder approval. A company may also become vulnerable to a hostile takeover as it can do little to prevent existing shareholders from selling their shares to investors that are attempting to acquire a controlling stake.

✗ **Demand:** as with bonds, if insufficient demand exists, a company may fail to raise all the capital it requires.

✗ **Costs:** profits must usually be shared between more people, although paying dividends is typically discretionary.

✗ **Administration:** share sales can be time consuming, complicated and costly to administer and once a company is publicly listed, it is subject to continuing (and at times onerous) disclosure requirements.

There are other factors that a company must consider when choosing between different methods of financing, including: its level of existing debt; the assets it has available to grant security over; any restrictions on its flexibility to borrow; its particular objectives; and current market conditions. These factors can affect the 'cost of borrowing', i.e. the size of the interest payments it will have to make to compensate a lender for the risk of giving the loan. Lenders may be unwilling to lend to riskier borrowers, or may only be willing to lend if those borrowers are willing to make high interest payments (lenders may feel that the risk is worth the potential for a high financial return).

Assets

- As discussed in the 'Security' section of this handbook, the extent to which a borrower has valuable assets over which security can be taken can determine whether (and if so, on which terms) a lender will be willing to lend.

Capital Structure

- The amount of debt a company has already taken on may affect the viability of different methods of financing.
- If a company has a high ratio of debt in comparison to equity, this means it is 'highly geared' and indicates it may lack sufficient assets to support debt repayments if additional debt is taken on. Lenders may therefore perceive highly geared companies as more risky borrowers and consequently charge them higher interest rates (or even refuse to lend them capital).

The Market

- **Demand:** if the value of a company is low, or it lacks a high profile or strong reputation, it may be unable to sell a sufficient number of shares or bonds at a price high enough to raise the required level of capital.
- **Market Conditions:** during an economic downturn, businesses in general perform less well (in part due to a decrease in consumer spending). This can reduce the willingness of investors to lend money at viable interest rates or invest in shares due to the increased risk of businesses becoming insolvent or underperforming.
- **Interest Rates:** interest rates are typically higher for borrowers with lower credit ratings. This is because lenders may demand a higher premium to compensate them for the increased risk of such borrowers defaulting. Therefore, debt financing may be less viable for companies with low credit ratings due to the potentially high cost of borrowing.
- **Banks:** issuing bonds may not be viable if investment banks are unwilling to underwrite the issue (which may be the case for firms with low credit ratings). In addition, banks may refuse to lend to firms lacking assets that can be used as collateral.

Credit Rating Agencies: these assess the likelihood of organisations or sovereigns being able to repay their debts. If a company has a high credit rating, its debt is perceived as a less risky investment and the company can typically borrow at a lower interest rate as a consequence. The main agencies that rate the credit of organisations and sovereigns are Moody's, Standard and Poor's and Fitch.

Restrictions / Flexibility

- A company's existing debt agreements and/or Articles of Association may prohibit it from taking on further debt.
- Existing shareholders may not approve a new share issue (a rights issue), especially if the company's earnings-per-share figure suggests that not enough profit is being generated to provide sufficient returns to all shareholders if additional shareholders are introduced. The company's Articles of Association may also place some restriction upon share issues.
- If businesses wish to remain flexible, issuing shares or bonds may be preferable as the terms upon which loans can be obtained from banks may be more restrictive. This is not always the case however, depending on the terms of a bond or share issue.

Articles Of Association: a document drawn up by the founders of a company at the time it is incorporated. It defines the duties, obligations, rights, powers and limitations of the company, directors, shareholders and other members.

Rights Issue: where existing shareholders receive the option to purchase additional shares, usually at a discount, in proportion to their existing shareholding. This option enables companies to raise new capital whilst affording existing shareholders the opportunity to retain the proportion of ownership that they had held before the new share issue.

Time Frame

- If a business requires short-term funding or immediate access to capital, taking a loan or using cash reserves may be preferable to issuing equity or bonds, which in contrast is generally a long-term commitment and can take a long time to set-up.

Basic Accounting & Financial Statements

In the UK, all registered companies are required to file financial accounts. However, publicly listed companies and private companies with a turnover exceeding £6.5 million are required to produce and publish more substantial, fully audited financial accounts. For investors, financial accounts may indicate the viability of different investment options. They provide an insight into a company's financial performance and financial standing. Financial accounts are thus the building blocks for an analysis of a company's ability to generate profit and meet interest repayments (for example, payments to banks that have lent the company money).

Some commercial law firms incorporate very basic financial accounts into the commercial case studies that they set during assessment centres and internships. Many commercial law applicants tend to underperform in relation to this element of interviews, but basic accounts are not difficult to understand and thus deserve some consideration. There are two key financial statements that commercial law candidates should aim to understand at the interview stage:

1. **The Income Statement:** this measures a company's revenue, expenses (including interest and taxes) and after-tax profit over a year; and
2. **The Balance Sheet** (or Statement of Financial Position): this provides a snapshot of a company's financial position at a particular date (usually the end of the year).

Note that the third key financial statement is the Cash Flow Statement, but this falls outside the scope of this handbook.

Income Statement

The Income Statement (known historically in the UK as the Profit and Loss Account) details a company's financial performance resulting from its day-to-day operations over a defined period of time (typically one year). It shows the income generated from a firm's operations over a period of time; the expenses relating to those operations; and the net profit (also known as the 'bottom line' as it appears at the bottom of the Income Statement). Different companies may report their Income Statements in slightly different ways. The below example provides a *very* simplified illustration of an Income Statement, including an outline of the key elements. Brackets have been used to indicate that the amount is to be deducted from the revenue/profit before tax figures.

Income Statement	
Revenue / Turnover / Sales	**£ XX.XX**
- Cost of Goods Sold	£ (XX.XX)
– Selling, General & Administrative Costs	£ (XX.XX)
= Profit Before Tax	**£ XX.XX**
– Tax	£ (XX.XX)
= **Net Profit**	**£ XX.XX**

📖 **Cost Of Goods Sold:** includes the direct costs associated with each sale made (usually variable costs). For example, if a firm sells 1,000 desks, such costs would include the direct costs associated with manufacturing each desk (e.g. the wood used).

📖 **Selling, General & Administrative Costs:** includes general expenses that do not directly relate to each individual sale (usually fixed costs). Examples include overheads such as office rental payments and utility bills and purchases of assets.

📖 **Net Profit:** refers to the amount of money remaining from the revenue after all related expenses have been subtracted

In case studies, candidates may be presented with basic financial accounts from the current year and the previous few years. If this is the case (depending on the issues you are asked to consider), start by analysing the profit figures to see how the company's performance has changed.

- If profits have increased year on year, this could indicate that the company could continue to thrive. Conversely, if the net profit has decreased, this could, on the face of it, suggest it may eventually run into financial difficulties. At this stage you should then try to discover (through looking at the accounts) *why* the net profit has decreased.
- For instance, a decrease in revenue (which could cause a corresponding decrease in net profit) could suggest consumers are purchasing less of the company's products, which in turn may indicate that new competitors have entered the market (or that existing competitors have developed a similar or superior product, perhaps at a more favourable price).
- If the revenue has remained the same or increased but the net profit has decreased, look at whether the costs have increased (which would also decrease the net profit). If costs have increased, does this suggest the company has failed to implement effective mechanisms to control costs (in which case think of potential solutions, for instance laying off staff or looking for cheaper suppliers?) or has the cost of raw materials increased (e.g. if the company produces apple juice, has the price of apples increased)? Alternatively, has the company made an investment (for instance purchased a factory) that has increased costs in the current year (and thus reduced the net profit) but may well contribute to an increase in net profit in future years?

lance Sheet / Statement Of Financial Position

The Balance Sheet (BS), also known as the Statement of Financial Position (SOFP), provides a snapshot of a company's financial situation. It lists the value of everything a business owns (its assets) and everything the business owes (its liabilities). All financial events in the life of a company must be accounted for through the recording of two corresponding entries in the Balance Sheet. Company assets (which form one side of the Balance Sheet) must have been supported through the use of some sort of financing (detailed on the other side of the Balance Sheet), either in the form of capital (equity) or through the company taking on debt (liabilities).

Asset: something of value to a company. Tangible assets include machinery and factories. Intangible assets include intellectual property rights, customer loyalty and knowledge. On a Balance Sheet, it is generally the tangible assets that are accounted for.

For example, if a company raises £1 million through selling shares and takes out a loan of £1 million when it first incorporates (starts up and registers as a company), its total assets will amount to £2 million.

- This £2 million will be recorded as:
  (a) £2 million cash in the 'Current Assets' section of the Balance Sheet; and
  (b) £1 million in the 'Equity' (share capital) section and £1 million in the 'Liabilities' section on the other side of the Balance Sheet.
- If the company subsequently purchases a building for £500,000, then cash (on the 'Assets' side) will reduce to £1.5 million and a new category will be created (also on the 'Assets' side), typically called Plant, Property & Equipment, the value of which will be £500,000.
- In the meantime, the Equity and Liabilities side of the Balance Sheet will remain unchanged as no new share capital has been received and no new debt has been taken on.
- If £500,000 of the loan is then paid off using cash, the 'Assets' section will decrease by £500,000 (to reflect the fact that cash has been spent on paying off the debt) and there would be a corresponding decrease in the 'Liabilities' section (to reflect the fact that the value of the outstanding loan has reduced to £500,000).

The Balance Sheet is essential when analysing a company's finances, as it contains information on the company's capital structure. There is a typical example of a Balance Sheet on the next page.

Capital Structure: this refers to the proportion of a company's capital (financial resources) that is attributable to debt and the proportion of the company's capital that is attributable to equity. This in turn can affect a company's ability to raise additional capital or its attractiveness to investors. For instance, a company that is highly in debt will be perceived as a riskier investment by potential lenders or investors.

Balance Sheet / Statement of Financial Position	
Assets	
Current Assets	**£ XX.XX**
Including cash, receivables (payments due from customers), inventory and other assets that will either be sold or removed from the Balance Sheet within a year.	
Non-Current Assets	**£ XX.XX**
Including machinery, buildings, long-term investments (including stakes in other companies) and other assets that will remain on the Balance Sheet for longer than a year.	
Total Assets	**£ XX.XX**
Equity	
Retained Earnings	**£ XX.XX**
Net profit minus dividends	
Share Capital	**£ XX.XX**
Capital received from issuing shares	
Liabilities	
Current Liabilities	**£ XX.XX**
Including short-term debt, payables (money owed to suppliers etc.), tax liabilities and other liabilities that will be removed from the Balance Sheet within a year.	
Non-Current Liabilities	**£ XX.XX**
Long-term debt and equivalents (e.g. pension liabilities) and other liabilities that will remain on the Balance Sheet for longer than a year.	
Total Liabilities + Equity	**£ XX.XX**

Introduction To Economics

This section is designed to give a very basic overview of some of the fundamental economics concepts that may be relevant for commercial law interviews and internships. It by no means provides a substantive account and far more reading, research and study is required to gain a solid grounding in the subject. Microeconomics may be of greater use when engaging in case studies, whereas macroeconomics may be of greater use when discussing current affairs.

Microeconomics: Supply & Demand

Microeconomics studies the interaction between buyers (consumers) and sellers (firms) and the factors that influence their decisions. It can provide an insight into the ways in which setting different prices for products will affect the quantity of products demanded (purchased) by consumers, which in turn can help sellers to determine the optimal price they should charge for products and the quantity of products that they should produce at that price to achieve maximum profitability.

Supply: the quantity of a product or service available for consumers to purchase at a specific price.

Demand: the quantity of a product or service that consumers are able and willing to purchase at a specific price.

If demand for a product increases to a greater extent than the supply of that product, firms may be able to charge a higher price for it. This is especially the case if there is an excess of consumers competing to purchase the product at a particular price. In such instances, whilst a price rise would inevitably deter some consumers from purchasing the product, the excess demand that had existed at the lower price indicates strong demand should still exist at a slightly higher price. However, if prices are increased too dramatically, demand may fall to a level that generates less profit overall than would have been generated at the original price.

Accordingly, for a company to generate optimal profit levels, a balancing act must be struck between generating as much profit as possible per individual sale and generating as many sales as possible. In contrast, if supply increases to a greater extent than demand, firms may have to reduce prices to increase demand (and thus ensure a greater number of products are sold overall). There are numerous elements that can affect supply and demand:

Price / Output

- Analysis of supply and demand trends can inform business decisions relating to the price at which products should be sold to consumers and the quantity of goods that should be produced by firms (firm output) at each potential selling price. This is because such analysis can provide an insight into the ways in which consumer demand (the quantity of sales made) will fluctuate at different price levels.
- Naturally, as prices increase, demand will usually fall, as fewer consumers will be able or willing to purchase the goods in question. For instance, a supermarket may sell 1000 apples in a day if they charge 30p per apple, but if the price charged were to rise to £1, the number of sales would likely decrease significantly. However, the way in which price affects demand varies depending on the type of product being sold.

Price Elasticity Of Demand: measures the extent to which price changes affect demand. Price-elastic products are products for which demand changes significantly in response to price changes. Examples include necessities (every-day household items) or generic items that can easily be purchased from other suppliers. Price-inelastic products are products for which demand changes less dramatically in response to price changes. Examples include luxury goods such as designer items, which are less easily substituted by other products.

Competing Goods

- Demand may be affected by the price of identical or similar goods. For instance, if Supermarket A sells their own brand of baked beans for 50p and subsequently Supermarket B reduces the price of its own brand of baked beans to 30p, demand will likely fall for Supermarket A's baked beans and increase for Supermarket B's.

Substitute / Complementary Goods

Substitute Goods: products that a consumer could purchase to satisfy the same purpose, need or want as a different product sold by another company. For instance, a train ticket may be a substitute for a plane ticket (if the route is similar) and if the price of rail travel drops, consumers may consequently decide to take a train rather than fly where possible.

Complementary Goods: products that can or must be purchased alongside another product. For instance, petrol is a complementary product to cars. If the price of petrol dramatically increases, consumers may (in the long term) be less inclined to purchase cars.

- Demand may also be affected by the price and availability of substitute goods or complementary goods. For instance, a fall in the price of a substitute product may increase the demand for that product and consequently reduce the demand for goods to which the substitute product serves a similar purpose.

- In contrast, a fall in the price of a complementary good may increase demand for products to which it is a complement, as the cost of the overall package will reduce.

Input Costs / Profit Margins

- The quantity of goods supplied may also depend on the input costs involved in producing the goods.

- If costs are low and the potential profits are high for a product, supply will likely increase as it is more beneficial for firms to produce and sell this product (existing firms may increase output and other firms may enter the market).

- If supply increases, firms may end up having to consequently compete on price in order to generate additional sales, resulting in the price decreasing for consumers.

Macroeconomics

Macroeconomics studies changes and trends in the economy as a whole at regional, national and international levels. It examines economy-wide phenomena such as changes in unemployment, interest rates, Gross Domestic Product, economic growth and inflation. A macroeconomic change in one area will typically have knock-on effects in other areas.

Bank Base Interest Rate: the interest rate at which national central banks lend money to domestic banks.

Inflation: the rate at which the prices of goods and services rise. When an economy experiences inflation, each unit of currency buys fewer goods and services. Inflation is the primary reason products cost more today than decades ago.

Aggregate Demand: the overall amount of goods and services demanded within a particular economy in a given period.

Aggregate Supply: the overall amount of goods and services produced within a particular economy in a given period.

Quantitative Easing: monetary policy used to stimulate economies. It involves central banks introducing new money into the economy by purchasing financial assets in the market. Flooding the market with additional capital in such a way leaves investors with additional funds, encouraging them to increase their engagement in investment activities.

Below is a simplified illustration of how central banks can influence GDP and inflation. We recommend that you research these concepts in greater detail.

Central Bank Base Interest Rate ↓
The central bank (e.g. the Bank of England) may lower its interest rate to achieve a particular economic policy goal.

↓

Commercial Bank Interest Rates ↓
Commercial banks (e.g. Barclays) react to changes in the base interest rate by altering their savings and loan rates.

↓

Spending ↑
Lower interest rates encourage consumers to spend more and save less because the return on their savings is lower.

↓

Investment ↑
Lower interest rates reduce borrowing costs, making it cheaper for firms to finance investment into new ventures.

↓

Demand for Goods & Services ↑
If spending and investment increase, this means more goods and services are being purchased (demanded).

↓

Employment & Production ↑
When demand increases, firms generally respond by hiring more workers and producing more goods and services to meet this increase.

↓

Gross Domestic Product (GDP) ↑
GDP refers to the total value of all the goods and services produced within a country during a given time period, which will thus rise.

↓

Inflation ↑
When demand for goods and services increases more than the supply, prices will increase and each unit of currency will buy fewer goods and services. The rate at which prices increase is called inflation. Inflation is the primary reason goods cost more today than decades ago.

↓

Exchange Rate ↓
Lowering domestic interest rates encourages investors to transfer their capital to countries offering higher interest rates (in search of a greater return on investment). To do this, investors sell the domestic currency and purchase the currency of the new country in which they wish to invest. When demand for the domestic currency decreases, the currency becomes less valuable and thus its exchange rate falls.

↓

Exports ↑
Exports increase, as a weaker exchange rate means domestic goods become more affordable for those purchasing with foreign currencies.

The Knock-On Effect Of Macroeconomic Change

Hawkish Signals: refers to the announcement of statistics (such as a greater than expected increase in GDP or inflation) that signal to investors that the central bank is likely to increase interest rates in response.

Dovish Signals: refers to the announcement of statistics (such as a greater than expected decrease in GDP, or deflation) that signal to investors that the central bank is likely to decrease interest rates in response.

Here are some examples of the ways in which investors may react to certain statistics or events. However, these are only examples and do not provide an objective indication of the ways in which all investors will react. For instance, some investment strategies may involve betting against the market, whilst the occurrence of certain events or changes in the economy may not necessary give rise to analogous investor interpretations or responses under different circumstances.

GDP is lower than expected

- This suggests the economy is weaker than predicted. Investors may therefore anticipate interest rate cuts in order to boost the economy.

Unemployment is much higher than expected

- This suggests overall demand for products and services (consumer spending) has fallen and as a result, less people are being employed to produce products and services.
- Investors may therefore anticipate interest rate cuts in order to stimulate spending and thus increase employment.

Inflation is much higher than expected

- This means prices may have increased by a greater amount than expected. This could be undesirable if it diminishes the value of the domestic currency by too great an extent (as each unit of the domestic currency will have less purchasing power).
- Investors may therefore anticipate an increase in interest rates in order to decrease spending (demand) and consequently stabilise inflation (or even trigger deflation).

An earthquake strikes a region

- Companies may be negatively affected by a large natural disaster. This is because, for instance, some businesses and consumers will have to spend their income on repairing or replacing assets, or may simply choose to spend less due to the uncertainty underpinning their region. In addition, transport links and other infrastructure (such as power lines) may well have been disrupted, which could hinder commercial activity.
- Investors may therefore feel less certain about the future of the region and may also expect the region's central bank to cut interest rates in order to encourage spending and investment. Consequently, investors may sell their investments in the region in order to reinvest in less risky markets and markets offering higher interest rates.
- All these factors could cause the region's home currency to depreciate. This is because once investors have sold their domestic investments, they will need to sell the currency that they received for the sale of these investments in order to buy the foreign currency required to make investments in other countries. This would increase the supply (and thus decrease the price) of the domestic currency.

A hurricane hits a major oil-producing region

- Investor concern could arise as to whether any damage caused by the hurricane would disrupt oil production and thus cause a shortfall in the supply of oil.
- Such a shortfall would likely result in oil prices increasing, which could reduce profits for companies dependent on oil.

Election results are released

- Investors may believe that a market-friendly candidate (a candidate likely to encourage investment and economic growth), post-election, will take action to stimulate investment in the region, therefore increasing the value of local market investments.

- If a market-friendly candidate in a country is expected to win an election, it is likely that the currency of the country will rally (increase in strength). This is because overall demand for that currency would likely increase, as investors looking to make additional investments into the country would require that country's currency to do so.

A corporate scandal / disaster occurs

- The share price of firms involved will likely plummet. This is because investors may feel uncertain about the potential negative effects a scandal or disaster could have upon the firm's costs, consumer demand or the firm's future in general and consequently decide to sell their investments (perhaps to reinvest in safer options in order to protect their capital).

Introduction To Microsoft Excel

This might seem like a bizarre section to include in a handbook focusing on commercial law. However, commercial lawyers use Microsoft Excel more frequently than you would expect. It can be an incredibly useful tool, particularly when it comes to compiling and sorting data and keeping records. For this reason, I have included a brief introduction to key Microsoft Excel functions and formulas below, just in case you end up using it during an internship. This is only a basic guide. To expand and deepen your understanding, Breaking Into Wall Street's 'Excellence With Excel' course is highly recommended. It is worth noting that slightly different commands and terminology may apply to different versions of Microsoft Excel (for instance, Microsoft Excel for Mac/PC, older versions and versions released in different countries). The information in this section relates primarily to PC keyboards and PC versions of Microsoft Excel. The screenshots in this section are used with permission from Microsoft.

Formatting

Number Formatting

- Microsoft Excel may sometimes format cells in ways that you do not intend it to. For instance, when inserting a date into a cell, instead of displaying 07/09/2015, Microsoft Excel may instead display the numbers in a different format. The same goes for decimals and percentages (etc.). You can ensure that cells display values as you intend them to by right clicking the relevant cell(s), selecting the 'Format Cells' option, then selecting your desired format. Cells will then update accordingly.

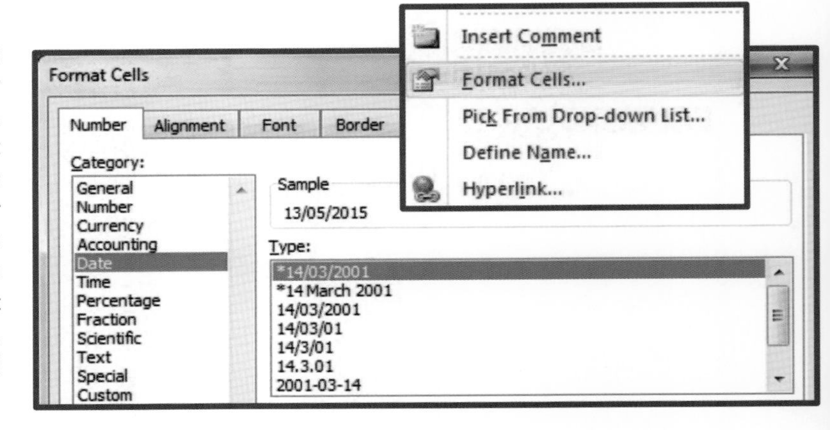

Sorting Data

- Microsoft Excel can make it easier for you to sort data (for instance, from smallest to largest if cells contain numbers, or in alphabetical order if cells contain letters). To sort your data, select the top cell of a chosen column and then click 'Sort' on the Data tab. This will give you different options for sorting your data.

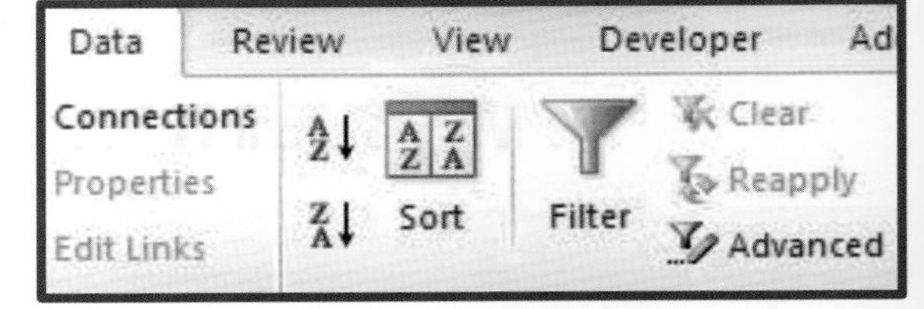

Hiding Columns / Rows

- The Hide function is useful if you want to display only the columns/rows in your worksheet that are relevant to your analysis. To hide data, select the column(s)/row(s) you want to hide, then right click and select Hide. To unhide those column(s)/row(s), select the columns/rows that are on either side of the hidden column(s)/row(s), then right click and select Unhide.

Freezing Panes

- Freezing panes can come in useful when your dataset contains hundreds of rows and/or columns and you need to reference a particular row or column regardless of where within the worksheet you are working. For instance, let us assume that the first row contains headings that specify which type of data should appear in each corresponding column. If you freeze the first row, no matter how far you subsequently scroll down, the entries in that first row will be displayed at the top of the area of the spreadsheet visible on your screen.

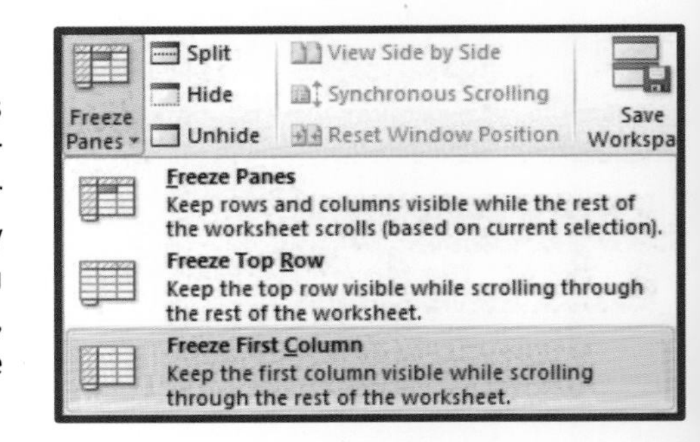

- To freeze a column or row, select the relevant column/row and then click Freeze Panes on the View tab. If you select an entire row, all the rows above it (not including the selected row) will freeze. If you select an entire column, all the columns to the left of it (not including the selected column) will freeze. If you select a particular cell, all the rows above it and the columns to the left of it will freeze.

Leaving Comments

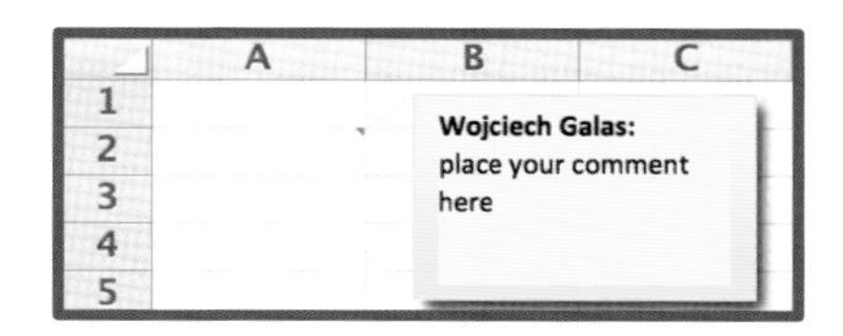

- It may be useful to leave comments in spreadsheets to ensure that other users can understand the contents. To do this, first select the cell to which you would like to attach a comment, then click New under the Review tab. A yellow box will open, giving you space to leave a comment. Once you have left a comment, a red arrow will appear in the top right corner of the cell to indicate to other users that upon clicking that cell, a comment will appear.

Graphs & Charts

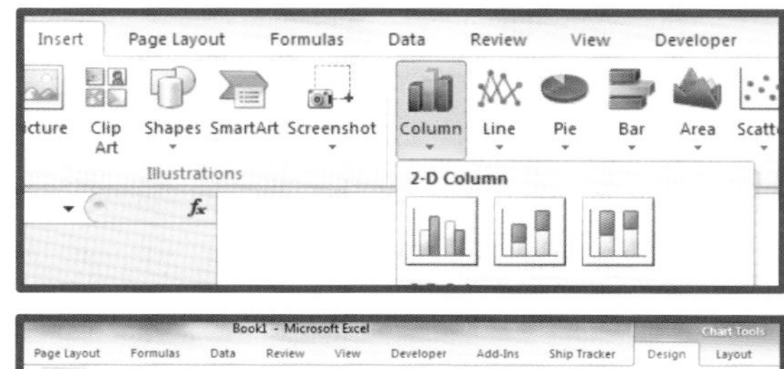

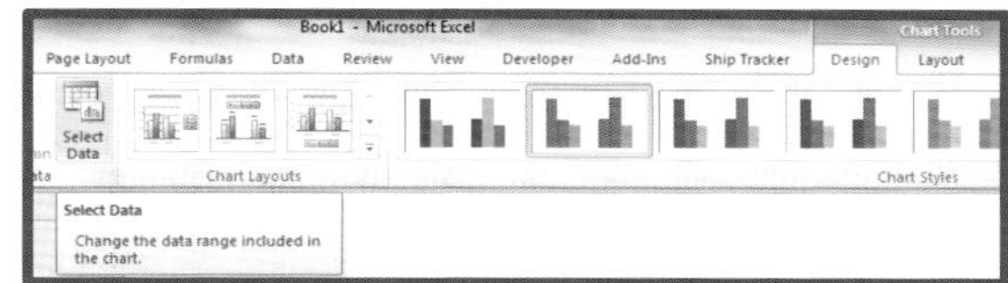

- Microsoft Excel provides a wide range of options for visualising data. To create a graph/chart, select the relevant data, then click the Inset tab and select the type of graph/ chart you would like to use (Column, Line, Pie, Bar etc.).
- Microsoft Excel tries to automatically determine which data should be displayed on the X-axis and Y-axis. If the data does not display in the way you intend it to once the graph/chart has been created, go to the Design tab under the Chart Tools ribbon and click Select Data. From here you can modify the way in which the graph/chart plots your data.

ɔrmulas

Inserting, Pasting & Moving Formulas

Selecting Cells

If you want to refer to particular cells in a formula/calculation, you can either type out the specific cell references that you want to include (e.g. 'A1') or click the relevant cells. You can also select groups of cells that you wish to include. You can do this by, for instance, typing in the start of the formula (e.g. '**=SUM(**') then clicking one cell and dragging the cursor across the other cells that you wish to include in the particular group. When you have finished dragging the cursor over the relevant cells and have let go of the mouse/track pad button, those cells will form a group. If you then want to refer to an additional group of cells into the formula, you repeat the same process (i.e. select the additional range of cells). The additional range of cells will form a second group and so on. A group of cells will display in a formula as two cell references separated by a colon, for instance 'A1:10'. **=SUM(A1:A10)** would sum A1, A2, A3...A10, whilst **=SUM(A1:B10)** would calculate *all* of the values in cells A1-A10 *and* B1-B10.

Pasting Formulas Into Different Cells

If you click and hold the bottom right corner of a cell that contains a formula, then drag the cursor down/across cells in the same column/row, the formula in the first cell will appear in each of the newly selected cells (relative to its new position). This function is applicable not only to formulas, but also to days of the week, months, numerical patterns etc. For instance, if you type 'Monday' into a cell and then drag the corner of the cell down, each subsequent cell will display the day of the week that follows the day displayed in the cell above. If you type '1' into a cell, '3' into the cell below, then highlight both cells and drag the corner of the bottom cell down, Excel will maintain the pattern of displaying only odd numbers in subsequent cells.

Calculations

=SUM(A1,B1,C1...) / **=A1-B1-C1...** **sum / subtract cell values**

=PRODUCT(A1,A2) / **=A1/A2** **multiply / divide cell values**

=AVERAGE(A1:A10) / **=MEDIAN(A1:A10)** **calculate the average / median of the specified values**

=COUNT(A1:A100) / **=COUNTA(A1:A100)** **counting the number of cells containing numbers / data**

- **=COUNT** enables you to calculate the number of cells in a specified range that contain any numbers. You can select the cells (including entire rows and/or columns) that you would like the formula to consider. In the above example, the formula would count the number of cells between (and including) A1 and A100 that contain numbers. Note that if you want to find the number of cells containing letters and/or symbols (or a combination of letters, symbols and numbers), replace **COUNT** with **COUNTA**.

General Interview & Internship Preparation

This handbook focuses primarily on the commercial knowledge required for commercial awareness and case study interviews. This section provides only a brief overview of the other elements that are most commonly found in interviews in order to provide you with some insight into the other preparation you should undertake before attending an interview. For in depth coverage of these elements, read the City Career Series: Application, Interview & Internship Handbook (more information on this is given on the inside front cover of this handbook).

Writing Applications & Preparing For Interviews

The recruitment process for City careers can involve an application stage, psychometric testing, a phone or Skype/video interview and an assessment centre at the firm's offices. These stages are designed to test your strengths, capabilities and suitability to the role for which you are applying. Other than the technical element already addressed previously in this handbook, there are four other key elements that firms tend to focus on when setting application questions and interviewing candidates. These are:

1. Competencies, Strengths & Experience
2. Career Motivation
3. Firm Motivation & Research
4. Current Affairs & The Legal Industry (another element of 'commercial awareness')

When preparing for interviews, I created separate documents for each of these elements and highlighted the documents on the morning of each interview, much like revising for an exam. All the elements tend to be relevant (at least to some extent) to most City interviews. Once you have covered these elements in detail, it should therefore take less time to prepare for subsequent interviews. However, ensure you tailor your preparation depending on the firm you are interviewing at (and the role you are applying for).

It is important that you never lie during interviews and that you are able to substantiate any statements you make. Recruiters are very skilled at noticing if you are trying to bluff your way through (you may be asked to provide a lot of detail when recounting experiences). Getting caught lying or overly-embellishing the truth reflects negatively upon your character and is likely to cause recruiters to question the other statements you have made. At the end of the day, they are looking to get to know *you*.

Throughout interviews, firms will in addition look for composure, confidence, clear articulation, strong interpersonal skills and enthusiasm. Try to keep calm and do not be afraid to disagree with interviewers, so long as you can justify your comments and are sure you are not objectively wrong!

Competencies, Strengths & Experience

- Firms will want to gain an insight into the skills and capabilities you have developed through your studies and extra curricular activities. Remind yourself of your personal experiences, positions of responsibility and extracurricular involvement. Focus on the skills and abilities you have developed.
- It is good to use a range of different examples in your applications and interviews, both academic and non-academic. This can help to demonstrate that you are a well-rounded individual. Try to demonstrate how your interests, experiences, competencies and strengths are relevant to the role for which you are applying and why they make you an ideal candidate. For instance, if you have worked in a supermarket, this could demonstrate work ethic, commitment and experience dealing with clients (clients are essentially customers), whilst evidencing that you have developed soft skills such as problem solving (if things have gone wrong) and negotiating.
- Helpful preparation can include listing out all the interesting and/or relevant experiences that you have accumulated. Include positions of responsibility you have held, societies and sports teams you have been involved with, interesting group projects you have undertaken at university, part-time jobs and work experience in industries relevant to the organisation to which you are applying. Consider the particular skills and strengths that could be drawn out of each. You should then be ready for competency-based questions.

We have supplemented this section with a series of videos and articles relating to answering competency and strengths-based questions. These can be found at:

www.CityCareerSeries.com → Applications & Interviews → Competencies

Key competencies for a successful lawyer

This isn't an exhaustive list of the qualities we want to see on an application form or at an interview at Freshfields, and every firm will be looking for something slightly different. But demonstrating these attributes effectively will help to set you apart!

Analytical ability. This is at the heart of what it means to be an effective solicitor. But what do recruiters really mean by this? Well, it's the ability to identify key issues, to explain concepts clearly, to think laterally, to argue and defend a point effectively, and to see both the big picture and the detail. Difficult to demonstrate on an application form? Not really – the Freshfields application form (with its 850-word personal statement) tests not only the content of your statement but also how it's assembled. Does your approach show a clear, logical mind? Are your reasons for commercial law not only convincing but also well put together? Are you not just smart, but smart in your delivery?

Commercial interest. At Freshfields, what we are really testing for is commercial interest, rather than simply commercial knowledge or commercial awareness. The latter may come from 10 minutes spent hurriedly with the *FT* before an interview. Commercial interest derives from a genuine curiosity about the commercial world around you – and we think that interest is difficult to fake. Have you ever thought about the way that organisations work and the concerns they have? Who runs them and for whose benefit? How their activities are financed? How they measure success and failure? What constraints there are on their growth? Who, if anyone, regulates them? That's commercial interest.

Interpersonal skills. The people we recruit must be sensitive to those around them, able to relate to different people well, to form good relationships with clients and to adapt well to the firm's ethos. So we are looking at your body language and eye contact. How do you describe your relations with others? How have you dealt with a difficult personal issue or what annoys you about other people? Through the (understandable!) interview nerves, can we see you developing the necessary self-confidence to win the trust of clients and colleagues? And, crucially, do you have a good sense of humour?

Determination and drive. We need people who can cope with the pace of life at Freshfields and the demands made of them by partners, clients and commercial life. We need highly motivated people who will be able and willing to devote energy to their roles and cope with a variety of demands on different jobs with flexibility and commitment. So we want to know how much you pack into your life, how proactive you are (do you lead or take the initiative, or do you just turn up?) and how you overcome difficulties? What do you get out of your studies and activities? What are you looking for in a job and what energises you?

Organisation and discipline. Freshfields lawyers must be organised in their approach to the massive deals and cases on which they will work; they need to be sure they have checked all relevant sources of information and that nothing is left to chance. So we are interested in how you organise your time. How do you prioritise between different activities? How do you know when you've done enough? We need to know that you can multi-task and that you can keep your cool.

Team playing. This is not just about playing in teams or working in committees. We need people who are interested in the common good and not personal glory – who may be leaders, but who will look after the interests of other team players, too. To what extent do you use 'I' as opposed to 'we'? Are you good at taking instructions and receiving feedback? Have you shown that you can get on with a range of people from different backgrounds?

For more information on what we are looking for and handy hints on the application and interview process, visit:

 freshfields.com/ukgraduates

 @freshfieldsgrad

 FreshfieldsGraduates

 @freshfieldsgrads

Firm Motivation & Research

- Firms will want to know your reasons for wanting to work for them. Research the firm at which you are interviewing in depth so that you are able to differentiate it from its competitors and explain why these differentiating factors particularly appeal to you.

- Do not give generic reasons for applying to that firm that merely reflect a quick skim of the firm's marketing materials. Think of legitimate ways to differentiate the firm and more importantly, relate these elements back to you in order to convince recruiters that these factors genuinely appeal. Which of your personal experiences have made the firm's culture, values, reputation and training structure appeal to you?

- You can access information on firms through a number of sources. You could start with the firm's website, its annual review, articles it has published and its profile on other websites. Follow the firm on Twitter, LinkedIn and Facebook and keep up to date with firm news relating to deals, poignant developments, awards and expansion plans. Sources such as The Lawyer, the Financial Times and the Economist can also be useful.

We have supplemented the above section with a series of videos and articles relating to firm motivation questions. These can be found at:

www.CityCareerSeries.com → Applications & Interviews → Motivation Questions

Career Motivation

- Firms will want to understand your motivation for pursuing your career of choice. Consider how your experiences have influenced your decision to pursue your desired career. Tell the story of how your interest in your chosen career has developed.

- For instance, when and why did your interest in your chosen career first materialise? Was it at school whilst studying a particular subject, whilst undertaking work experience, or following a conversation with an acquaintance working in that industry? What did you do to further explore this interest (e.g. undertake certain work experience)? How did your research confirm that this was the right career for you? Ensure your answer is sensible however. Stating that you have always wanted to be a lawyer may not come across as genuine and believable to your interviewer!

We have supplemented the above section with a series of videos and articles relating to career motivation questions. These can be found at:

www.CityCareerSeries.com → Applications & Interviews → Motivation Questions

Current Affairs & The Legal Industry

- Firms may want to see evidence of your interest in and understanding of current affairs and the industry you are looking to work in. Build up your knowledge and understanding of current affairs to evidence your interest in the wider economy. Relate your knowledge to your prospective employer, its clients and the markets in which they operate. You should also research the challenges the industry is facing and assess proposed solutions.

- If there is a particular topic that is consistently discussed on the front pages prior to your interview (for instance, regulation, tax avoidance, political instability, elections, disasters, emerging markets, whether Scotland should become independent, whether England should remain in the EU etc.), then try to gain some insight into the topic before the interview. There is every chance the interviewer will bring it up.

- In addition, check the front page of the Financial Times on the morning of your interview just in case something major has happened. A topic that comes up fairly often in some way or another is the challenges facing the Legal industry. You may for instance be asked what challenges the firm is facing, or what you would do if you took over the firm today.

- There are many other sources you can use to build your awareness, knowledge and understanding of current affairs. BBC Business News (online) provides a concise and straightforward account of current affairs. Helpfully, there are usually links at the bottom of articles to related articles.

- Reading these can help you to build a more comprehensive understanding of different topics. The Financial Times and the Economist similarly provide an overview of the most relevant topical issues affecting the business and finance world.

- Some sources let you subscribe to useful 'daily digest' summaries of key news articles, which can really help to keep you abreast of what is going on in the business world. Consider following well-known commentators and publications on Twitter, delving into blogs focusing on financial services, reading client alerts published by firms and searching out YouTube videos focusing on particular topical issues.

We have produced a series of articles analysing a variety of different industries. These can be found at:

www.CityCareerSeries.com → Commercial Awareness → Industry Analyses

We have produced a series of articles explaining and analysing topical current affairs. Read these at:

www.CityCareerSeries.com → Commercial Awareness → Topical Current Affairs

We produce weekly topical news summaries, which can be viewed at:

www.CityCareerSeries.com → Commercial Awareness → Headlines

Subscribe to our mailing list to receive these news summaries by email. You can do this at:

www.CityCareerSeries.com → Connect → Sign Up

Challenges facing the legal industry

How the legal industry has changed, how it will continue to develop and what the key challenges are for law firms.

If you want a job as a lawyer you'll need to be able to demonstrate that you know something about the industry you're entering. The good news is that in many respects the challenges lawyers face haven't changed that much over the last decade or two. The bad news is that what used to be the preserve of partners are now things that even young lawyers are expected to attempt: understanding the client's viewpoint; winning new business; managing how the work is done and the impact of that on price; delivering client-focused solutions not just legal advice; being able to work in a team and on occasion showing leadership skills.

But first the big picture stuff. The Bar (if you want to be a barrister) is shrinking. It is as hard as ever to get pupillage, let alone a tenancy. High street practice has polarised between the small one-and-two-partner general practices (ultimately probably doomed) and bigger, multi-location chains that are beginning to attract third-party capital through ABSs (alternative business structures). The threat from what once was called Tesco law (in practice pioneered by the Co-op until it hit its own problems) has not materialised in quite the way expected. Instead, third-party funders of litigation have swept to the fore.

Regional and national practices (often with overseas offices) serve wealthy individuals and local and national businesses. International corporate, commercial and financial practice is dominated by the global law firms. The biggest have at their heart US/UK capabilities but with offices in the most vibrant parts of the global economy – Asia, China and the emerging markets of South America and Africa.

Clients for their part shop around. They often use more than one and go to specific firms for specialist expertise. They also negotiate over price. When appointing firms they make them 'pitch' for the business (show the client why they should get it, including flexibility on price). So price is something you need to be aware of. In the old days lawyers charged by the hour. But that's an open-ended commitment on the client's side that rewards the least efficient lawyer who takes the most time. Now clients expect fixed prices.

But for a law firm to offer a fixed price it has to be steeped i the type of work on offer and know where the issues (that c throw out a fixed price) are likely to arise. The key is understanding the way in which work is done and delivere and making it as efficient as possible. This is called 'proces and increasingly law firms are adopting project manageme techniques to make sure that work runs according to cours and everyone in a team knows what they should be doing, why and when, and how it all inter-connects.

This means that, although lawyers need to be able to work teams, they also need to take individual responsibility for aspects of the process. This is where leadership comes in. Traditional leadership is someone in charge issuing orders Modern leadership is almost the opposite. It's team membe putting their hands up to assume personal responsibility fo certain aspects, owning those tasks and seeing them throu to completion in a way that complements what everyone el is doing. Teamwork makes it harder to hide. If you don't do your bit, everyone else is let down. The way young lawyers make their careers is by assuming responsibility, knowing when to seek more senior help, being resilient in the face o demanding deadlines and taking the initiative rather than waiting to be asked.

If you have a good grasp of these things, of teamwork, of process and its impact on price, and you understand the client's concerns, it means you have a good story when you come to pitch. Business development is really about identifying clients' needs and then showing them how you can meet those needs. The key is being able to quiz clients about their business or circumstances and explain how the firm can help them, with concrete examples of benefits (called value-adds) provided to other clients in similar situations. Hiding behind the law and not being prepared t enter the client's world doesn't work any more (if it ever di It's a tall order.

And what can you look forward to if you can demonstrate a of this? A fantastically rewarding career, full of intellectua challenge and satisfaction.

Christopher Stoakes is the author of All You Need To Kno About Commercial Awareness, All You Need To Know Abo The City and Is Law For You? He was formerly Director of Knowledge and Learning at Hogan Lovells.

GUIDE TO PREPARING FOR INTERVIEWS

Know yourself

- Review what the firm is looking for (their competencies). Do you have good examples to talk about for each one?
- Review your application form. Especially if you made lots of applications and/or it was a while ago. At Ashurst, the content of your application forms the basis of your interview.

Know the firm

- What is their position in the market?
- Who are their clients, core practice areas and competitors?
- SWOT away the stress: have you thought about the firm's strengths, weaknesses, opportunities and threats?
- Check out recent news. Any rumblings of game-changing mergers, big client wins or partner hires?

Know why you want to work for the firm

- Do you know why you are applying to that firm? If you do not, you will come unstuck. Remind yourself why they meet your career criteria.
- Think about the commonalities between the firms you have applied to. Can you identify from them the sort of firms you're attracted to? If you are struggling to find similarities, then you might need to re-think.

Think about your presentation and how you come across

- Dress professionally; your interviewer will want to be able to picture taking you to a client meeting a few years down the line.
- You will be nervous, that is to be expected, but think about your body language. Tone down the ear-scratching, arm-waving, hand-rubbing, as this will distract your interviewer.
- Maintain eye contact and smile; this will help you to remain calm and composed.

Know what you want to get out of the process and what questions to ask at the end

- Questions at the end are for you but can impress too. Ask about the future of the firm, the strategy, and hot topics at the partner conference.
- You will probably get to meet a trainee so use them to get under the skin of the firm's culture. Ask them about their last really great day, their worst and the support they receive.

You can't prepare for everything

- Most firms will be looking to see how you perform under pressure and will test you on topics you likely won't have been able to prepare for. Do not panic; take your time, do not be afraid to be wrong, try to think around the issue and remember that sometimes the obvious answer is the right one.
- You might be asked your opinion on an issue. Can you defend your position and will you accept that you may be wrong? Don't be afraid to hold your ground if you can back up your argument.

We have opportunities for all law and non-law students and graduates – from first year to final year and beyond.

Applications open on 1 September for our winter vacation scheme, summer vacation schemes and our first year programme, Ahead with Ashurst.

Applications open on the 1 October for September 2021 and March 2022 training contracts. Closing dates vary and we recruit on a rolling basis.

Please visit our website for more information.

Begin now at www.ashurst.com/careers

AshurstTrainees

Converting Internships Into Full-time Jobs

Approaching The Work

- If you cannot do the work to the standard expected by the firm, they will be unlikely to offer you a job. Whilst some pieces of set work will be harder than others, and minor mistakes may be completely fine, general attention to detail should never be overlooked. Proof read your work multiple times (even ask colleagues to have a read if you think this might be appropriate) and make sure there are no spelling, grammatical or formatting errors. These can be easily avoided.

- Check to see whether there are particular fonts, templates or settings in Microsoft Word or Excel that firms use as part of their 'house style' and where possible, adhere to these. This demonstrates your ability to absorb (and work in a way that aligns with) the ways in which the firm operates, whilst also ensuring the people judging your work will approve of it stylistically. There may also be templates of contracts that you can edit rather than having to start from scratch. Research and/or ask. You could also see whether the firm has an intranet and/or support departments that can help (e.g. Knowledge Management departments).

- Consider the intended recipient of the work. If it is for a client, then ensure it is short, concise and to the point (unless you are told otherwise) and that the language is not too technical or full of jargon and acronyms. If the work is for a senior employee, perhaps query whether they would like you to reference the work (this means indicating the sources from which you found the information included), whether they have a rough word limit in mind, whether they would like a printed and/or an electronic copy and perhaps even whether they would like single or double sided printing. These are not stupid questions and can help to ensure the work is perceived as favourably as possible.

- Whenever you meet with someone, bring a pad and pen so that you are ready to write down instructions if you are set a new piece of work. Once you have received the instructions, you could summarise them back to your supervisor to check that you have understood them correctly. Ask questions if you are unclear on a particular instruction, but listen carefully. Asking the same question twice will waste your supervisor's time and reflect negatively on you. Try to figure out as much as possible by yourself through researching carefully. You could try to list out questions that arise as you run into difficulties and then ask them all at once when your supervisor has a free moment. Repeatedly interrupting your supervisor every time you have a question could frustrate him or her and disrupt his or her own work.

- Keep a work diary as you go along. You will then be able to reflect back on your previous work if questioned by your supervisor or an interviewer at a later stage. However, do not forget about confidentiality. If you include confidential information in your work diary, then consider refraining from taking it outside the office (during or after your internship). You could alternatively include just enough information to jog your memory about what you were doing, without including confidential client information. When making a job application after completing an internship, never include confidential details of work completed elsewhere. This could call into question your ability to adhere to the required standards of confidentiality.

Demonstrating Your Motivation

- You are selling yourself during an internship as much as a firm is selling itself to you. Your personality will therefore influence a firm's inclination (or not!) to hire you. They will look for genuine commitment to your chosen career, as they would rather not invest in you, only for you to leave a short way into your career. They will look to see how well you fit in with the firm's culture. Do you get on well with the firm's existing employees? They will look to see whether you are a hard worker. Have you asked around for work if your supervisor has nothing for you, or have you avoided responsibility or failed to show a genuine interest in the work?

- Your behaviour will influence whether a firm believes you have the ability to complete work in a very demanding, client-led environment and whether you can be trusted to work with high-profile clients and professional services firms that expect only the very best from their advisors and colleagues. Some roles may also require ample confidence and presentation skills. If this is the case, think about whether you are the quiet person in the corner, or the person making an effort to get involved and socialise and how this could in turn reflect on your ability to fulfil the role for which you are applying.

- If you have not received enough work, then request more (you could offer other departments a hand if appropriate). Remember, everything is a learning opportunity, so do not complain if you are set boring or repetitive tasks. You will inevitably receive such tasks at the start of your career if you end up working for the firm in the future. Avoid looking as if you would not be prepared to pitch in and get things done.

Group Work & Team Presentations

- Many City careers involve employees having to regularly work in teams. This may be internally within their particular departments; internally within their firm but with a number of different departments that have a role on a different aspect of a deal (for instance the tax or regulatory implications of a transaction); with employees working within a different office within the global network of offices (if the firm is international); and/or with other types of firms. For instance, many transactions involve input from investment banks, commercial law firms, accountancy firms, consultancy firms, regulators and institutional investors and these different industry players must coordinate effectively in order to successfully execute the transaction at hand.

- Internships (and some assessment days) typically include a team-based exercise to test the way in which candidates interact with others on a mutual task. This could involve completing a creative task in a group, for instance building a Lego tower in line with specific instructions. It could involve researching and delivering a group presentation relating to the firm in general or a particular department. This may be structured as a pitch to a fictional client that focuses on the firm's capabilities, its past experience, the challenges it is facing, the locations in which new offices should be opened, or even the way in which it can offer value for money to clients (perhaps addressing fee structures or value-adding services). Alternatively, group exercises could involve engaging in fictitious commercial negotiations (sometimes with more than 2 opposing sides) or discussing various investment options as a group before agreeing which one to pursue. These exercises may also be designed to test candidates' commercial awareness and knowledge of the firm.

- Graduate recruiters are very perceptive and are likely to notice if the attitude of one or two candidates adversely impacts upon the team dynamic (even if this dynamic only surfaces when candidates are working together in private). Try to work well with team members. Encourage quieter team members to speak, be receptive of ideas (or constructively contribute to ideas you believe are less strong). You could try to link ideas together and draw on others' contributions, arrive at meetings on time and having completed your delegated work and above all, avoid being rude, overbearing or competitive. Candidates who are outwardly competitive are not generally looked upon favourably. Such an attitude can indicate that candidates will negatively impact upon the firm's culture if they were to be offered a job. After all, these exercises are about collaboration, not competition!

- Many presentations are followed by question and answer sessions. If you have worked on a presentation in a team, then make sure you know each other's work and research inside out. You may be allowed to defer an answer to a colleague, but equally you may be expected to answer questions on your colleagues' work. If you are clearly familiar with each other's input then this provides an indication to your assessors that you have worked effectively as a team. You may also want to consider supplementing a presentation with a handout. This can enhance your presentation and make your group stand out, whilst also demonstrating creativity, effective teamwork and strong organisation. However, perhaps consider giving out the handout after your speech as it may otherwise distract those in the room from what you have to say.

- Many graduate recruiters claim that there are enough jobs available for a majority of internship candidates if they are all good enough at the work and a strong enough fit for the firm. Acting competitively during group exercises is more likely to lose you an offer than help you to secure one!

Enthusiasm

- One of the pieces of feedback that many rejected candidates receive after an internship is that their enthusiasm for the firm was lacking. It is easy to assume that if you are clever enough to do the work that the role will require you to do, then surely this should be enough. However, if you do not seem enthusiastic when spending only a few weeks (or months) at the firm, this could give the impression that 6 months or a year down the line, perhaps you will no longer care at all. This could in turn affect the quality of your work, impact negatively upon the teams you work in and adversely affect the culture of the firm. Firms will be less willing to hire someone who may potentially negatively impact the firm's culture. Firms generally perceive their culture as something that keeps employees motivated (and thus from a commercial standpoint, boosts productivity). It's not difficult to smile for a few weeks!

- In addition (although this is merely an opinion and is not necessarily reflective of the way all firms operate), firms may be less willing to make offers if they do not believe candidates will accept. This is partially due to the fact that it will be harder to recruit the required number of people (e.g. schedule the right number of interviews or make the right number of offers) if the firm has no idea how many candidates are likely to accept their offers. A lack of enthusiasm may indicate a candidate will quit after only a short period at the firm, meaning that the money invested in training them throughout an internship and the early stages of their career will be wasted.

- You can demonstrate enthusiasm simply by getting involved in as much as you can. Ask lots of carefully considered questions (to your supervisors, graduate recruitment, people you meet during socials and people that give you presentations). Asking questions can really help to demonstrate your genuine interest in the firm.

- Attend as many social and networking events as possible (although of course do not let this affect the quality of your work if you are facing tight deadlines and avoid drinking too much alcohol!). Attendance at these events can demonstrate your interest in integrating into the firm, getting to know your potential future colleagues (including other interns and existing employees) and contributing to the firm's culture.

- Repeatedly avoiding such events could indicate that you would perhaps rather be working elsewhere, or that you have little interest in familiarising yourself with the firm's employees or its culture. This in turn may also reflect negatively upon your interest in networking (a skill that is essential to facilitate effective team working, especially when external parties are involved) and your motivation for working at that particular firm.

- However, if there are any cultural circumstances that impinge upon your ability to socialise to the same extent as others (for instance if, during Ramadan, you are due to open the fast at the same time that a social is taking place), then explain the situation to the graduate recruitment team.

Professionalism

- Be open and approachable. Try to meet as many people as you can. This could mean asking to sit in another division for a few hours or simply going for coffees with members of your team.

- Be professional and reliable. It should go without saying, but be punctual (especially following a social event that ended late). Do not be too informal, as this could be mistaken for arrogance. Check what the dress code is before you arrive and remain smart and presentable (even if some of the employees take a more casual approach). This does not necessarily mean you must ignore casual Fridays for instance, but do not show up in shorts and flip-flops simply because you have seen a Partner or Director do so.

- Remember you are making an impression on the entire firm. Treat everyone with courtesy and respect, whether they are your supervisor, the receptionists, the most senior employees at the firm, the secretaries or the cleaners. You are being assessed at all times and you never know who graduate recruitment will approach for an opinion on you throughout/after the internship.

- I have heard stories of interns talking negatively about other interns, not realising that one of the group to which they were speaking happened to be a good friend of that intern from university. Any animosity caused in such a manner can typically be perceived by graduate recruiters, which in my personal experience has not done any favours for those speaking negatively of others. Your fellow interns may well be your future colleagues so treat them well in order to ensure that a positive working relationship ensues in the future.

- I have heard candidates at times talk negatively about other firms to graduate recruitment representatives, presumably intending to demonstrate that the current firm is their preference. This could be a huge mistake. Firstly, bad mouthing other firms could convey a degree of arrogance and suggest that you lack professionalism. Secondly, graduate recruiters tend to move between firms fairly regularly and may well end up at the firm that you were badmouthing before that firm has made their final decision about whether to offer you a job.

- Two of the graduate recruiters running the final internship that I undertook had worked at other firms at the same time that I had attended open days and internships at those other firms. One had even looked after me on my interview day at a different firm only 5 months earlier! Moral of the story? Be careful what you say to your colleagues and to graduate recruiters. Remain professional and do not talk negatively about other people and firms - it does not reflect well on you!

Final / Fast-track Interviews

- Whilst three or four structured reasons for wanting to work at a particular firm may scrape you through an interview to secure an internship, much more may be expected of you in an end-of-internship interview. Having spent a number of weeks immersed in a firm's culture, meeting many employees and engaging in real work, your reasons for wanting to work at the firm will have to be more personal, more substantive and less reliant on graduate recruitment marketing materials.

- Ask yourself whether there was a similar type of personality within the firm. Were there people you particularly enjoyed meeting? Was there a culture that really resonated with you (if so, describe this culture and why it appeals)? Were there pieces of work that you felt were particularly interesting and indicative of the type of work that the firm carries out? Did you attend a presentation on the structure of the training that helped to differentiate the firm from its competitors or suggested that the firm's approach to developing its employees aligns with your preferred means of learning and developing?

- Be ready to discuss the work you have completed in detail and how this work fits in with the wider context of the firm's operations. Prepare some carefully considered questions for your interviewers. These might relate to the firm's culture, its future strategies, the challenges it is facing (or may face in the future), its training or anything else you can think of that demonstrates your genuine interest in working there. If you do ask about the firm's challenges and future strategies however, make sure you have undertaken some related research as you may be asked to express a personal opinion.

- Be prepared to give feedback. What have you enjoyed? What did you not enjoy? How does the firm compare to other firms you have interned at? Has your opinion of the firm changed since your internship commenced? If so, how? What has differed from your expectations and preconceptions?

We have supplemented this section with a series of videos relating to converting internships into full-time jobs. These can be found at:

www.CityCareerSeries.com → Internships → Converting Internships

Further Reading

Christopher Stoakes is the author that inspired me to set up City Career Series and write this handbook. As a former financial journalist, City lawyer, management consultant and top trainer, he knows the business and financial worlds inside out. His engaging style and ability to explain complex concepts with surprising simplicity meant that his books played a significant role in helping me to prepare for interviews. As such, I strongly recommend that you supplement your study of this handbook by reading some (or all) of the books detailed in this section.

Understand the financial markets

Anyone who works in business these days needs to understand the financial world. All You Need To Know About The City is the best-selling guide that students and young professionals use to get up-to-speed quickly and painlessly. It uses the simple analogy of a market to explain who the participants are (issuers, intermediaries and institutional investors). It looks at what they buy and sell, from shares and bonds to foreign exchange, derivatives and securitisations. It examines the lifecycle of a company and the anatomy of a global bank. It explains why interest rates change and how they drive markets. In short, it enables you to understand the financial markets with no prior knowledge.

Enhance your commercial awareness

If you want a job in the business world you need to be commercially aware. What is it and how do you get it? All You Need To Know About Commercial Awareness tells you. It explains what matters to businesses, how they are funded, the importance of cash flow, the purpose of strategy and the quest for customers. It explains how companies are organised and what they are looking for when you apply for a job. This book contextualises much of the information within this handbook, providing an excellent supplementary read.

Write well at work

A majority of firms require candidates to submit written assignments as part of the interview and/or internship assessment process. Candidates are expected to write concisely and accurately and frame their words within a clear and coherent structure. However, employers complain that young people can't write. What are they looking for and how can you deliver it? Get To The Point explains how. Writing well in the workplace is critical to your career. Words are still the principal form of communication between people in business. Write well and you will shine. Write badly and you could torpedo your career.

Want to become a lawyer?

Articulating your motivation for wanting to pursue law, both as a degree discipline and as a potential career, is something with which many students tend to struggle. However, firms are increasingly expecting candidates to provide strong, substantial and genuine reasons to support their decision to pursue law. Is Law For You? provides a strong insight into the world of law through explaining both what lawyers do and the many avenues of specialisation they pursue. Whether or not you eventually decide to become a lawyer, law is a critical underpinning to business and thus having a basic grasp of the law will give you an edge regardless.

We have produced some additional resources to help you build your commercial awareness. These can be found at:

www.CityCareerSeries.com → Commercial Awareness → Developing Your Commercial Awareness